THE
FOLKLORE
OF TREES

*To my wife, Hannah, who helped weave
my thoughts together and gave me the time
to write. And to Edwyn and Ivor,
our beautiful distractions.*

THE FOLKLORE OF TREES

The fascinating stories
behind nature's guardians

AIDAN MEIGHAN

Leaping Hare Press

Contents

FOREWORD

Some of my best friends have been trees. They are deeply rooted in the story of my life: the middle-aged oak that supported the nest holding the kestrel chick I fell in love with as a teenage boy; the trusty yew in the wood that shelters me and my dogs from mid-walk downpours; the home-grown hazels, alders and rowans whose progress charts another trip around the sun; the magnificent beech under which my cremated carbon will one day be returned. The list goes on…

We all have stories to tell about our favourite trees, but I've often wondered what tales trees could tell us. If only they could talk! Those millennium-old woody relics, which survive to witness the very best and worst of humanity, and some of which are older than written communication itself – a fact that leaves me speechless.

Whilst we wage wars under olive branches, selfishly execute gentle giants just to improve a view and sacrifice entire forests for fuel, trees remain, for the most part, humanity's benign life supporters. That's perhaps why I was drawn to the pages where the author recounts the deadly superpowers of yews (p. 143), before unfurling their remarkable folklore. I love the idea of falling asleep under a gnarly old yew and being resurrected a year later to dance with supernaturals… but only if they come in poodle form!

Mostly, though, it was the romance of being finally returned to dust that appealed to me. Much as I love life, sometimes I cannot wait to be scattered, along with the ashes of my beloved dogs, under the boughs of my best friend: that sacred beech pollard in the heart of our woods.

The Folklore of Trees is an exquisite and entertaining read with wonderfully diverse, memorable tales begging to be retold around the dinner table, by the office desk, at bedtime… or out and about under the listening trees. This book reminds us of the enduring power of stories to connect us to our history, to nature and hopefully to an ever-greener future. We need to love life, we need to love trees.

Chris Packham

INTRODUCTION

Trees of every shape and size imaginable grow across our planet, effortlessly intertwining with the cultural identity of the people who share their landscape, while nourishing growing civilizations beneath their shade. Trees make history. Date palms in the deserts of West Asia and coconuts on the islands of the Pacific offered lifelines to early settlers and, when these civilizations prospered, their trees were revered in literature and folklore. The trade of frankincense and fine silk (produced by the mulberry-reliant silkworm) led to the formation of the spice and silk trade routes. This sparked an explosion of trade and cultural exchange between the East and West and set the humble wild crab apple of Kazakhstan on its journey to become the iconic apple we know today.

As well as shelter and sustenance, trees give us stories. Storytelling is in its infancy compared to the existence of trees, but it is as old as humankind, long pre-dating the written word. Folklore enthrals, educates and bestows core cultural beliefs and traditions upon new generations, and for as long as these tales have been told, trees have been main characters. Arboreal motifs and symbols feature in many sacred texts, as well as the oldest surviving written story, the Mesopotamian *Epic of Gilgamesh*, where the cedar forests of Lebanon represent the divine realm – a place of great and sacred power.

Many traditions – such as those of the Aboriginal communities of Australia and American Indians – are not written down. Nature itself is imbued with spirituality and teachings, and the stories and wisdom are passed down orally from one generation to the next. These stories are more fluid, evolving and often highly personal. The historic mistreatment of these communities has led to some understandable trepidation about sharing their stories and knowledge. The ultimate priority must be to preserve their cultural identity and avoid misrepresentation or further exploitation. Including stories from these communities in this book seemed essential as I believe it is from their long and harmonious existence with trees that we can probably learn the most.

Stories of trees ground us. Before cathedrals and skyscrapers, people looked to living landmarks for answers. The Mesoamericans, Europeans and people of West Asia all adopted 'world trees' to quantify their existence on Earth: trees that with their canopies brush the heavens, build bridges with their branches and twist their roots down into the underworld through the soil of existence. The Norse Yggdrasil (ash), Maya Yaxche (kapok), cosmic Hindu Vat Vriksha (banyan), Hungarian Égig érő fa and Turkic Ulukayın all represented life in its entirety and the axis mundi – the connecting point between all realms of existence.

Both trees as a whole and their separate parts are symbolic. The fruits, leaves and seeds of trees take on different meanings across cultures. For example, the apple – or forbidden fruit – carries the baggage of original sin, lust and death, but is also thought to represent love, knowledge and immortality. In contrast, the olive branch is a syncretic symbol of peace.

For the ancient Greeks and Romans, trees were imbued with symbolism and often associated with specific gods and nymphs. Many of the trees mentioned in this book feature in the Roman poet Ovid's *Metamorphoses*, where a cast of characters undergo dramatic transformations into trees, transferring to them their personalities and characteristics.

The shared symbolism between these mythological figures and their corresponding trees or plants were evident in the four alternating Panhellenic games (Olympics, Pythian, Nemean and Isthmian). Each of these games were dedicated to a god and the victory wreaths were chosen accordingly. The olive wreaths of the Olympics were associated with Zeus, laurel was awarded at the Pythian games in honour of Apollo, pine wreaths at the Isthmian games for Poseidon, and wild celery was presented at the Nemean games, also affiliated with Zeus.

The Paganism of the Celts was based on a reverence for nature, and trees were a cornerstone of their rituals and beliefs. The term 'druid' likely derives from the Irish–Gaelic word for oak tree, 'doire'. Even their language had its foundation in trees: in the Druidic Ogham alphabet – also known as the 'tree alphabet' – many of the letters (known as 'fews') are represented as trees. Words constructed from these letters (known as 'feda' (trees)) are read in the manner of climbing a tree, from bottom to top: each letter is identifiable by the number of 'flescs' (twigs) on the way up. *Auraincept*, an Old Irish text from the seventh or eighth century, explains:

> Right of stem, left of stem, athwart of stem, through stem, about stem. Thus is a tree climbed, to wit, treading on the root of the tree first with thy right hand first and thy left hand after. Then with the stem, and against it and through it and about it.

Another example of the link between trees and language is Bríatharogaim – old Irish kennings. These poetic two-word explanations of the Ogham alphabet elaborate on the characteristics of individual trees. For example, the willow's kennings translate as 'pallor of a lifeless one', 'sustenance of bees' and 'beginning of honey'.

All major religions celebrate trees in their teachings. There is Islam's Lote Tree of the Utmost Boundary, Buddhism's sacred tree of enlightenment, the Hindu peepal tree where Brahma, Vishnu and Shiva dwelt, and the Christian tree of knowledge (and first sin). Many Christian traditions practised today have Pagan origins and were remodelled to align with Christian values, such as the beloved traditions of the Christmas tree, yule logs and holly wreaths – all adapted from the winter solstice festival of Yule.

The influence of trees on humanity is profound and so it stands to reason that they are celebrated in folklore across religion and culture. Peering through the leaves gives us a unique perspective on the connectedness of humankind throughout time. The similarities are as prodigious as the differences – with individuals from different centuries worshipping different gods in contrasting landscapes, yet sharing uncannily similar stories about their arboreal friends.

The Folklore of Trees is a collection of stories about trees that ultimately tell stories about us. Our relationship with trees is one that needs to be nurtured, now more than ever. Trees can survive without us, but we cannot survive without trees.

ADANSONIA

BAOBAB

This deciduous giant is one of the most bizarre trees in this book; when its leaves drop in winter it looks, as the British explorer David Livingstone remarked, like 'a giant upturned carrot'.

Of the eight species of baobab, six are endemic to Madagascar. The other two species can be found in Australia and Africa, having somehow crossed the huge expanse of open ocean, only to become extinct from whence they came.

Baobabs can live a thousand years or more, and older specimens are often hollow on the inside. Their stout, cavernous trunks provide sanctuary for animals and humans alike, offering makeshift homes, churches, pubs, toilets, stores, reservoirs and even prisons.

In both African and Australian folklore, there are numerous origin stories to explain the baobab's confused appearance. It varies in subject matter from ungrateful hyenas and wandering trees to frustrated gods who overturned it in a fit of pique.

One African folk tale tells that long ago there lived a beautiful tree who never lost its flowers. It drank greedily through its mighty roots, was plump with gluttony and smug from root to crown. There came a terrible drought, and the only water that remained was inside the vain and over-gorged tree. The thirsty animals and wilting plants begged the tree to share the water, but it refused. In desperation, the animals joined together to uproot the tree. They pulled and pulled until the great tree was ripped from the ground, flying into the sky before landing crown first. The once vain tree wept a deluge of tears on account of its now ugly appearance, allowing the savannah to grow lush and green again.

The baobab has evolved to make the most of any downpour, as its trunk swells to store water. This talent has given it the nickname 'bottle tree' and during droughts the Kalahari bushmen will tap its trunk and drink the sap through grass straws. In Madagascar, lightning-struck trees have been repurposed as reservoirs.

In fact, a lot of the tree is edible or useful to humans: the seeds make an effective coffee substitute, the fibrous bark can be refined into ropes, cloth and baskets, and extracts from the tree are used in traditional medicines. The baobab has the rare ability to regrow bark, which means that with sustainable harvesting the tree can offer its bounty for many generations. However, an African superstition cautions against picking baobab flowers, as doing so will 'lead the lions to you'. As with many such superstitions, this serves as a warning against exploiting the tree too greedily. It is wiser to let it fruit and take only what you need.

In Senegal, the trees are used as tombs for the Griot people. Griots, famed for their history-keeping and mastery of words, believe that if you are buried, so too is your knowledge. So the deceased are entombed within a baobab so that their knowledge can diffuse through the tree. The chosen tree is then rewarded with the protection of the Griot ancestors.

Fallen baobabs are mourned by locals and ceremonies are carried out in honour of their passing. Much like the oak, baobabs are celebrated for their individuality. Each has its own unique character, appearance and stories. Here are just a few examples:

- **Baobab amoureux (*A. rubrostipa*)**, Malagasy savannah, Madagascar: According to Sakalava legend, two forbidden lovers were promised to others in their respective rival villages. Heartbroken, they pleaded to the gods. Touched by their devotion, the gods immortalized them as the intertwined baobabs amoureux.
- **The Hillgrove lockup (*A. Gregorii*)**, Wyndham, Australia: Non-Aboriginal police adapted the hollowed tree to operate as an overnight lockup in the 1890s for Aboriginal people being escorted for sentencing. The entrance was bored into the tree's internal cavity with its foreboding (and now very faded) name etched into the trunk.
- **The prison tree (*A. Gregorii*),** Derby, Australia: This famed tree owes its name to a transposed misappropriation from the lesser known Hillgrove lockup (see above). Within this baobab is a large chamber that is about 4 m (13 ft) wide, and while there is no evidence that it was ever used as a prison, bones found within it suggest it was used as an ossuary of the dead by the Aboriginal Nyikina and Warrwa people.
- **Chapman's tree (*A. Digitata*)**, Makgadikgadi Pans, Botswana: British explorers David Livingstone and James Chapman both used this tree as a navigational beacon in the nineteenth century, and it served as the first post office in Africa. Travellers heading north would leave letters for those heading south to collect and take to the shipyards of Cape Town, bound for home. This venerable beauty fell in 2016.
- **Avenue of baobabs (*A. Grandidieri*)**, Morondava, Madagascar: Known locally as *renala*, meaning 'mother of the forest', this beautiful and impressive parade of baobabs is now a must-have photo for tourists around the world, but once these trees would have been a small part of a dense forest.

ALNUS GLUTINOSA

BLACK ALDER

The alder tree is a swamp-dwelling giant that 'bleeds' when cut and has deep roots that turn as hard as stone in the riverbed, harbouring mysterious hidey-holes that are favourites with otters. It seems folkloric by nature. The alder does not just resist water, it is strengthened by it, making it the perfect wood for bridges, locks and shipbuilding. Famously, Venice is built on alder, and its role as a 'bridging tree' is a theme oft-repeated in folklore.

Alder woods or 'carrs' can be eerie places; these marshy woodland impasses were considered a suitable hideout for malign fairies, boggarts (mischievous folklore creatures who reside in swampy area) and also outlaws, some of whom, including the bow-and-arrow-wielding Robin Hood, used dye obtained from the catkins to camouflage their clothes.

In Irish folklore, it was believed that passing an alder on your travels was a bad omen, perhaps because of the 'Red man' or *Far Darrig*, a short, pugnacious fae (fairy) who played 'gruesome' tricks on travellers crossing rivers and marshlands. The legendary Irish hero Fionn mac Cumhaill met such a character – 'a low-sized, reddish man that was standing in the middle of the river' – in *The Daughter of King Under-Wave*, but was fortunate enough to be carried over the water in the palm of his hand rather than tricked or harmed.

This idea of a giant who provides passage over water perhaps links the character to Brân the Blessed, who features in Welsh folklore, particularly the second branch of the *Mabinogion* (twelfth- to thirteenth-century Welsh prose). Brân was the personification of the alder, a giant known for his ability to bridge rivers. When Brân heard that his sister, Branwen, was being mistreated by the Irish king, he embarked on a rescue mission, walking across the sea ahead of his fleet of ships. When Brân and his followers encountered an impasse in the river, where the (likely alder) bridge had been destroyed by the Irish, he said 'he that would lead, let him be a bridge. I will be a bridge', and laid himself from bank to bank so his followers could cross over him (the proverb endures today).

In the *The Black Dog of the Wild Forest*, a Romani story first captured in writing by Francis H. Groome in 1899, a young prince tried to flee on horseback on his sixteenth birthday in order to escape a prophesy that he would be killed by a monstrous, fire-breathing dog. As is usually the case, fate would not be denied and a black dog started to pursue him. Along the way, two hags offered him sanctuary and gifts: two dogs of his own and an alder rod. They told him:

> hit this rod in the water, and a fine bridge will jump up. And when you get to t'other side, just hit the water, and the bridge will fall in again, and the Black Dog of the Wild Forest cannot get you.

To the prince's delight, the rod worked, conjuring bridges for his escape – until he missed a tap and his pursuer was upon him. The black dog nearly killed him, but with the help of his own two hounds, the prince defeated his nemesis and returned home. As he neared his parents' castle, his hounds transformed into two beautiful women and the three lived happily ever after.

In the Ogham 'tree' alphabet, alder (*fearnóg* in Irish) represents the third letter, *fearn*. Old Irish 'kennings' are poetic two-word explanations of the Ogham alphabet, with each letter having three surviving kennings. Alder's kennings describe the significance of the tree, which is itself reflected in Irish mythology:

♦ *Comét lachta* (**milk container**): Alder wood is a favourite of carpenters. Soft, when dry, it does not split easily, has anti-microbial properties and was widely used for making pails and other dairy equipment.
♦ *Dín cridi* (**protection of the heart**): The Celts used alder wood to make shields for their warriors, as it was believed to have protective spiritual properties, offering both physical and mental fortitude. The wood's reddish sap led to the belief that it 'bled', and that the warriors who bore it would not have to.
♦ *Airenach fían* (**vanguard of warriors**): Often associated with war, alder is a 'pioneer species' (like birch and rowan) known to arrive first in habitats. In the obscure fourteenth-century poem 'Battle of the Trees' (*Book of Taliesin*), Alder formed the vanguard, leading the trees of Britain into battle against the king of the underworld. King Conchobar mac Nessa's Red Branch knights were likely named after its properties of strength and protection.

BETULA PENDULA

SILVER BIRCH

The silver birch was affectionately dubbed the 'Lady of the Woods' by the poet Samuel Taylor Coleridge, who thought it the most beautiful of forest trees. With its striking, papery white bark, dark, corky gnarls and weeping branches clad in lime-green or yellow-gold leaves, it is certainly a gorgeous specimen, although not immune to spooky stories – it is known worldwide as the tree of witches, specifically because it traditionally provides material for their brooms.

The trees also play important roles in Celtic cleansing and renewal rituals, likely reflecting their behaviour in the natural world. Wind-pollinated birches are often the first trees to establish themselves in barren landscapes, colonizing the thawing plains after the last Ice Age, on lava flows or atop a disused quarry. They do so by braving the bitter cold and using their mighty root networks to draw nutrients back to the surface, paving the way for the pines and oaks that later shade them out. The root system at the birch's base gives life to mushrooms – the fruiting bodies of mycorrhizal fungi – that enjoy a mutually beneficial relationship with the tree.

Birch, like spruce, has a particularly strong relationship with *Amanita muscaria* (fly agaric), the hallucinogenic mushroom used in 'soma', an ancient Vedic 'drink of the gods'. The mushroom's potent mind-altering properties may have inspired fairy tales and literary classics – most famously kickstarting Alice's trippy adventures in Wonderland in the books by Lewis Carroll – and influencing Christmas traditions (*see* NORWAY SPRUCE, p. 105). Other fungi found beneath birches' dappled shade include the birch milkcap, birch brittlegill, birch knight and, on the tree itself, birch polypore – also known as razor strop (on account of its leathery flesh used to sharpen tools). The aptly named witches' broom fungus, which grows on the branches of silver birch trees, causes the branches to proliferate wildly in dense 'broom-like' thickets. These were said to grow in trees that witches had passed, or rested in, and were an indicator of nearby supernatural forces. In Scandinavia, the fungally fashioned besoms could be hung above your bed to relieve nightmares and sleep paralysis – after all, there is nothing more relaxing than the silhouette of a witch's broom over your head.

A witch's broom is one of the most iconic artefacts folklore has to offer. Often the besom is made of birch and the broom handle of willow (*see* p. 129), but the legendary Slavic witch Baba Yaga and the many witches of Somerset in England are said to have fashioned the brooms entirely from silver birch.

The origin of the witch's broom likely began with the use of the besoms to cleanse sites before rituals. Fly Agaric, often growing beneath silver birches, was a popular ingredient in witches' 'oyntments', 'brews' and 'salves', along with other botanicals such as deadly nightshade, henbane and mandrake.

During the Middle Ages, it was discovered that these mind-altering concoctions could also be absorbed through sweat glands or mucus membranes, bypassing the intestinal anguish caused by oral consumption. How they applied the hallucinogenic oils may account for why witches sit astride broom handles. According to the fifteenth-century theologian Jordanes de Bergamo, 'on certain days or nights, they anoint a staff and ride on it to the appointed place or anoint themselves under the arms and in other hairy places'.

As well as being used by witches for their spells, birch was also employed to repel evil spirits. For example, during the festival of Samhain (the predecessor of Halloween and the start of the Celtic new year, when the connection between the living and the dead was at its strongest), birch twigs and besoms were used to brush away lingering malign spirits from the past year.

Up until the late nineteenth century, a tradition in the English county of Herefordshire saw birch branches wrapped in white and red ribbons and leant against stable doors to prevent witches from stealing the horses and joyriding them throughout the night, returning them with knots in their manes and tails – a practice known as 'hag-riding'.

Other folk stories include a Scottish old wives' belief that herding a barren cow with a birch branch could make it fertile, and the unlikely idea that no person had ever been struck by lightning when standing beneath a birch. In Wales, newlyweds would jump over a birch branch lain across the threshold of their new home; if they opted to step rather than jump, the bride could expect immediate conception. Also in Wales, the tree had associations with courtship. Walking in pairs beneath its boughs was thought to encourage a good love match, and tokens fashioned from birch were offered as gestures of intent.

Centuries earlier, in ancient Rome, birch was a symbol of authoritarianism. Bundles of birch rods bound together to form a handle of an axe known as 'fasces' were carried around by magistrates' henchmen. The name and symbolism was adopted in the early twentieth century by Mussolini on forming the Fascist party in Italy.

BOSWELLIA SACRA

FRANKINCENSE

Frankincense is a gnarled and winding tree with roots that anchor it into cracks in the limestone valleys of Oman, Somalia and Yemen. It is both charming and tenacious, with beautiful blooms and a tendency to grow on sheer, jagged cliffs. It weeps fragrant sap, sought after by collectors, who leave it to set into a resin before selling it as incense. At times its weight has been valued more than that of gold.

The use of frankincense is documented as long ago as the fourth millennium BCE, when the ancient Egyptians used it to embalm the dead and cleanse the living. Their *Book of the Dead* described it as 'the sweat of the gods, fallen to earth'.

During antiquity, thousands of tonnes of frankincense crossed South Arabia to be traded in Greece and Rome every year. This trade led to the domestication of the camel and contributed to the formation of one of the greatest trade routes in history. The Frankincense Trail and the Incense Route eventually connected with the Silk Road (*see* APPLE, p. 85), bringing frankincense to a near-global market.

The trade routes were melting pots for sharing folklore, and stories evolved with every re-telling. Occasionally, rivalry between traders directed the narrative, with Yemeni incense traders spreading fear-mongering rumours of flying serpents that swarmed the canopies of the resinous trees to scare away other traders. This tall tale was probably inspired by a real snake, *Echis pyramidum*, a stealthy, saw-scaled viper known for its leaping strikes and venomous bite. The trees' serpent-like web of branches likely enhanced the association.

Another association is with the phoenix, a legendary bird originating in ancient Egypt. The phoenix was said to nest in frankincense trees, feeding from the flowers and slaking its thirst on the sap. When the phoenix grew old, it would surround itself in sprigs of frankincense and cinnamon and self-combust, rising again from the ashes. (In other traditions the phoenix is associated with DATE PALM, *see* p. 101.)

According to ancient Omani legend, the frankincense tree was once a djinn (a spirit who can assume human or animal form) who fell in love with a human boy. The love between the djinn and the boy was forbidden by her kind. To stop her from acting upon her heart, she was transformed into a frankincense tree. The djinn stayed that way, weeping fragrant tears for eternity.

Roman writer Ovid gives us another origin story for the frankincense tree in his poem *Metamorphoses*. The story starts with the sun king, Sol, who was betrothed to the goddess Aphrodite. Sol, discovering Aphrodite's affair with Ares, humiliated her in front of the other gods. A furious Aphrodite sought revenge by manipulating the devotions of Sol, and set his heart upon a beautiful Persian princess, Leucothoe. The Sun King fell completely in love with her, but his carnal temptation was so strong that he schemed to gain entry to Leucothoe's chambers in the form of the queen, before returning to his own form to rape her. Unbeknownst to him, this was observed by Clytie (a water nymph in Ovid's account; Leucothoe's sister in others). In a fit of jealousy, Clytie, who was herself in love with Sol, told the king what she had seen, omitting Leucothoe's protests.

The king was enraged by the scandal. He ignored his daughters' anguished cries that the act was unbidden and buried her alive. Scared and desperate, the princess prayed, hands outstretched, for Sol to rescue her. Sol, still besotted with her despite his brutal act, answered and melted the sand away from her face, only to find himself too late and the princess already dead. Bereft, he honoured her by pouring a fragrant nectar around her body. Then he harnessed the power of the sun to make things grow, and created the first frankincense tree, in her memory.

Throughout time, frankincense has been used in worshipping rituals, burned to honour gods of many faiths. Most famously, its remarkable resin was one of the gifts carried by the Magi (Three Kings) in the Bible. Balthasar gave the baby Jesus frankincense, perhaps to show the world that he was indeed the Son of God.

♦ Jesus was not the first to receive the famed giftset of gold, frankincense and myrrh – the Macedonian Greek general Seleucus I Nicator may have set a precedent in 288/7 BCE when he offered them (and other gifts) to Apollo in the temple of Didyma.
♦ Frankincense typically smells earthy, woody and honey-like, with a hint of citrus and pine.

CEDRUS LIBANI

CEDAR OF LEBANON

In the past, large areas of West Asia and the Eastern Mediterranean basin were covered in vast swathes of cedar forest. Civilizations such as the ancient Egyptians, Assyrians, Babylonians, Persians and early Christians considered it a valuable resource, with historical and symbolic resonance.

The immense cedar forest of Lebanon sets the scene for the oldest surviving literary work of all, the *Epic of Gilgamesh*, written on clay tablets over 4,000 years ago in ancient Mesopotamia. The text was rediscovered in 1839, at which point its influence on the *Iliad*, the *Odyssey* and the Bible's Old Testament became abundantly clear.

The *Epic*'s titular hero, Gilgamesh, and his accomplice, Enkidu, journeyed through the forest to reach the Mountain of Cedar. As they approached it, they heard bellowing from above as Humbaba, the ogre-giant and forest guardian, launched a volley of insults and threats at them. The two men, thirsty for fame and glory, slayed the giant and began to fell the unguarded trees, cutting an especially large trunk from which they intended to build the gateway to the temple of Enlil (the supreme god), as well as enough wood to make a raft that would carry it home along the Euphrates.

Much of the history and folklore surrounding cedar regards it as a valuable commodity for building temples, ships and even sarcophagi for some very famous pharaohs. Sadly, this has led to a long history of over-exploitation and deforestation. During the construction of the First Temple of King Solomon in Jerusalem in the Bible, he summoned 80,000 lumberjacks to cut the necessary wood. This workforce of biblical proportions denuded the thick blanket of forest, laying bare the mountain beneath.

In 118 CE, the Roman Emperor Hadrian attempted to protect the great cedar forest so that he could reserve the wood for his own fleet, while in 1876, the British Queen Victoria commissioned a stone wall to surround the sacred trees and protect them from young goats. Later, during the Lebanese Civil War (1975–90), Druze militants laid land mines around forests in the Chouf mountains to prevent them from being cut down. Sadly, there is no protection from rising global temperatures, and climate change is taking its toll on the forest, moving it further and further up the mountains. In what is now a UNESCO World Heritage site called Ouadi Qadisha, only 400 trees remain.

Reforestation efforts continue in Lebanon, and luckily the tree still lives on in other countries. In Britain, the first cedars arrived in 1638, when Edward Pococke, chaplain to the Turkey Company at Aleppo, successfully germinated a seed that he had brought back from Syria. The exotic tree went on to adorn many stately gardens, particularly after the mid-eighteenth century, when the famous landscape architect Capability Brown used them extensively in his designs.

One cedar in Bretby Hall in Derbyshire, England, was said to be a harbinger of death in the resident Carnarvon family. The trees are known to drop their girthy horizontal branches on a whim, but when this specimen did so the family paid close attention, after several coincidental deaths were observed as its branches fell. After Lord Carnarvon's discovery of Tutankhamun's tomb in Egypt's Valley of the Kings in 1922, one of the boughs from the Bretby

Hall cedar dropped. Lord Carnarvon's celebrations after unearthing the boy king, whose body had been embalmed with cedar oil inside a gilded cedar wood casket, were short-lived. In 1923 he died of sickness related to a mosquito bite, strengthening the bizarre superstition.

In other folk rituals, burning the tree is believed to invite poor luck, with Arabs believing that to damage a cedar summons grave ill-fortune. As we have seen from its history of over-exploitation, this is true for no living thing more than the species itself, but hopefully the ongoing conservation efforts will successfully preserve this most majestic of trees.

♦ In 1986 a 2,000-year-old cedarwood fishing boat was recovered from the Sea of Galilee, the region where Jesus, son of God and founder of Christianity, was known to have lived. Although it is relatively unlikely to have a direct connection, it was dubbed 'the Jesus Boat'.

♦ There are a staggering 103 mentions of cedar in the Bible, including this from Psalm 92: 'The righteous shall flourish like the palm tree: he shall grow like a cedar in Lebanon.'

CEIBA PENTANDRA

KAPOK

The dramatic kapok, ceiba or silk cotton tree towers as high as a twenty-storey building, casting shade with its large horizontal branches. The young, green trees are covered in thorns and the long-lived centurion trees support their colossal height with buttresses. Flying on the wind and taking to the seas, the seeds travelled from tropical America to the west coast of Africa 13,000 years ago. Although a 'tree of life' for the Maya civilization, much of the folklore warns us away from the kapok, a shadowy hiding place for malevolent beings and blood-sucking witches.

It is reported that Christopher Columbus anchored his ship, the *Santa Maria*, to a large kapok tree, known as *La Cieba de Colón* (The Columbus Tree), in 1496. This event, in what is now the Dominican Republic, marked the inception of Santo Domingo, considered the oldest European city in the New World. The Europeans arrival had a profoundly damaging impact on the Taíno people, who had a long-standing relationship with the kapok.

The Taíno believed the tree was the home of the spirits of the dead, the *opías*, and that it was also associated with the deities of the underworld. At night the *opías* would leave the trees to eat the guayaba fruit (guavas), much like the bats that roost in kapoks and feast on the same.

Kapok trees have nectar-rich flowers that bloom and attract bats before the leaves develop. The menacing thorns on its trunk, however, deter any further visitors and serve as mini reservoirs that help the trees resist drought. These thorns were popular motifs in Maya art.

In Mesoamerica, gods, goddesses and all living things were categorized as belonging to the north, south, east or west. Each direction carried different spiritual meanings and served to guide the lives of the people. For the Maya, the centre of it all was the *Ya'axché* (green tree) or kapok, their tree of life and axis mundi. Its large, flared roots, known as buttresses, sprawl out in the different directions, while the trunk represents the middle world and the meeting point of an additional fifth and sixth direction. The roots penetrate the underworld, and the great canopy reaches into the celestial levels to support the heavens above.

In Trinidad and Tobago, there is a folk legend of a huge kapok, deep in the forest, called 'The Castle of the Devil'. It is said that a local carpenter carved seven rooms into the trunk before luring Bazil, the Demon of Death, into it. From then on, vampiric, shape-shifting *soucouyant*s (witches) would shed their physical forms at night and hang them from the branches before going to suck blood from humans; their harvest shared with the resident Demon of Death.

The partitions between buttresses are believed to be a favoured hiding spot for *douens* – short, mischievous sprites who wear straw hats on their faceless heads and stand on backwards feet. The *douens* lure children into the forests by mimicking their parents' voices, but they are not all bad, as they also aid Papa Bois, keeper of the trees, in protecting the forest.

If *douens* and the devil were not enough, the flared roots are also said to be the hiding place of La Diablesse, a seductress who lures men in with her beauty, before altering her posture to reveal a muscular leg and cloven hoof, with which she kicks them over a cliff edge.

Since the kapok tree originated in the Caribbean before taking root in West Africa, there has been an exchange of folklore. In fact, much of it started in West Africa and then travelled in the other direction with African enslaved people travelling to the Caribbean. One story tells of the witch, Gang Gang Sara, who made the journey herself. Because she never ate salt, Gang Gang Sara had the gift of flight, which she used to fly to Jamaica to find the family stolen from her by the enslavers. She found them and other enslaved Africans and met her husband, Tom, there. When her husband died, Sara decided to fly home to Africa and climbed a giant kapok to take off. However, when she jumped, she found she could no longer take to the air and plummeted to her death. The salt that she had eaten in Jamaica had made her too heavy to fly. Gang Gang Sara and Tom's headstones remain a popular tourist spot in Tobago today.

♦ In Burkina Faso, West Africa, kapok wood is used to make Bwa masks. Crafted by skilled carpenters and spiritual leaders, often while in a trance-like state, the masks are worn for many different rituals.
♦ In Sierra Leone, the tree has become a symbol of freedom, thanks to returning enslaved African Americans, who gathered and prayed under the branches of a kapok in the capital Freetown after the American War of Independence. This tree of liberation fell to a storm in 2023.
♦ There was a Caribbean belief, popular in the nineteenth century, that kapoks would take nightly walks so that they could commune with one another.

COCOS NUCIFERA

COCONUT

Many millions of years ago, the palm family (*Arecaceae*) branched in two directions. Inland palms evolved into the date palm, while those along the coast evolved to produce coconuts. Having originated in Malaysia and Indonesia, the coconut's range now spans Earth's equatorial belt thanks to its seaworthy and buoyant fruit.

Austronesians – a group of peoples originating in southeast Asia and migrating far and wide – became the most successful seafarers of their time, thanks to the humble coconut palm. Rope from the husks and wood from the trees were used to construct their vessels, while the coconuts themselves allowed seafarers to voyage further, supplying a neatly packaged and long-lasting source of food and water.

In the Philippines, it is believed that coconut trees are the reincarnation of people who want to continue serving their community. One Old Filipino myth speaks of the palm tree that brought life to Earth. Three deities lived in isolation, each believing themselves alone in the universe, Bathalà (the supreme god), Ulilang Kaluluwa (snake spirit of the sky and clouds) and Galang Kaluluwa (the winged cosmic travelling head). One day, Ulilang Kaluluwa was bored and went to the mountains. To his surprise he met Bathalà. When they *both* introduced themselves as the 'supreme' being, a fight ensued. Bathalà won and the snake was killed.

Soon after, Galang Kaluluwa, the cosmic flying head, appeared to Bathalà. He was more amenable, and they became good friends. Bathalà explained that he longed to create people for company, but the barren land had nothing to sustain their mortal life. Eventually, Galang sickened. The flying head asked Bathalà to be buried with the snake, as he had one last gift to give. The sole surviving god obliged and, to his joy, a tree sprouted from the shared grave – the trunk in likeness to the snake god's body and the leaves like Galang's wings. Bathalà observed three holes in the fruit and realized it was the very picture of Galang's face. The palm tree provided food, drink and shade, finally allowing Bathalà to fulfil his dreams and create humankind.

In Samoa, it is an eel that morphs into a palm tree. The eel sees a girl bathing and falls in love with her. When his love is unrequited, he begs the girl to decapitate and bury him. From his long body grows the trunk of the coconut palm and in an ultimate proclamation of his eternal love, he produces the coconut, a divine gift to be enjoyed by the girl and all future generations. The three holes of the cocunut represent the eyes and mouth of the love-struck eel.

The 'stretching tree' in Hawaiian folklore is used in a boy's search for his father. His mother sang to the coconut, often referred to as their ancestor: '*Niu ola hiki*/Oh life-giving coconut, *niu loa hiki*/Oh far-travelling coconut.' Her song brought a new tree from the earth. She told her son to climb on and continued to chant, the trunk stretching out to sea as she did so. Eventually the crown of the tree settled on far-off Tahiti and the boy clambered down, reunited with his father.

Since coconuts made long-distance travel possible, seafarers were able to take them around the world. Malay and Arab merchants traded them in Africa, the Caribbean and the Atlantic coast of America, and wherever the trees took root, they insinuated themselves into the culture, nowhere more than the southern Indian state of Kerala, which translates from Malayalam as 'land of coconuts'.

According to the mythical origins of Kerala, the verdant state was created when Parashurama (sixth avatar of Vishnu) threw his axe, bloodied by the massacre of King Kartavirya and his many warriors, into the sea. Where it landed, the sea recoiled and the land of Kerala was formed, but it was barren and salty. Parashurama asked Nagaraja Vasuki, the serpent king, to spit on the land and make it fertile. Parashurama then created the coconut palm but Brahma (god of all creation) criticized him for overreaching. Parashurama agreed to stop as long as Kerala could keep the coconut and honour Nagaraja by allowing snakes to protect the land.

- Throughout India, coconuts are part of the daily offering to the gods. Each part of the coconut can have a different meaning – a broken one reflects self-sacrifice, and one without the husk represents a relinquishment of the outer ego.
- The coconut palm is also called the tree of life, the tree of heaven, and the tree of abundance, and to Hindus, is known as *Kalpavriksha* – the tree that provides all necessities.
- In Keralan folklore, a hapless fisherman is gifted the ability to leave his head ashore by a local magician, allowing him to fill his body with fish as he swims in the sea. When a curious boy buries the fisherman's head on shore, the head grows into a coconut palm, and his body is transformed into a fish.
- The tree's Latin name derives from the Portuguese and Spanish word 'coco', which means skull or head, and *nucifera*, which translates from Latin as 'nut bearing'.

CORYLUS AVELLANA

HAZEL

Hazel trees and their small, round nuts have been a valuable source of protein, protection and prediction since Neolithic times. The wood, a versatile material for tool-making and construction, is also thought to ward away darkness and witchcraft. The nuts and shells can be burnt to make romantic predictions, and eaten to increase knowledge and wisdom.

Hazel also seems to have snake-repelling properties. According to the popular fifth-century legend, it was a hazel wand that St Patrick used to drive away all the snakes from Ireland. The Brothers Grimm told a story about a mother who, when foraging strawberries for her child, stopped in her tracks when she saw an adder approach – she dived behind a nearby hazel for cover. When it was safe again, she collected the berries and declared that 'as the hazel-bush has been my protection this time, it shall in future protect others also'. Accordingly, hazel crosses and rings of hazel have been used to protect against adder bites and even cure them.

Circe, the powerful enchantress from ancient Greece, wielded her hazel wand against Odysseus's men, turning the lot of them into swine after they ventured on to her island. The messenger god, Hermes, stepped in, giving Odysseus a special flower that offered immunity from Circe's spells. She was forced to surrender to Odysseus's sword, reverse the curse and allowed them all to live on her island for a year.

Hermes and his Roman counterpart, Mercury, both carried the *caduceus*, a magical hazel staff entwined with two snakes and a pair of wings, now a symbol of modern medicine. It bestowed them with the power to put people to sleep and wake them again, as well as pacify turbulent situations.

In Somerset, England, there is an old phrase, 'Plenty of catkins, plenty of prams', indicating that abundant displays of hazelnut catkins were thought to pre-empt a baby boom. The nineteenth-century British MP William Cobbett even noted that 'a great nut year is a great bastard year', reasoning that the more nuts there were to pick, the more young nut pickers would indulge in frivolous behaviour. Girls were advised not to go nutting on a Sunday, as it might bring about a diabolical conception come their wedding night.

The romantic predictions did not stop there. A pair of hazelnuts carved with initials could be used to test compatibility on All Hallow's Eve. Nuts that smouldered slowly on the coals indicated a trouble-free marriage, but a tumultuous response might predict a rocky one. A jumping nut meant infidelity, but a nut with a fierce blaze reflected the gentleman's passion.

The hazel tree owes its name to the Anglo-Saxon term *haesel knuts* (hatted nuts), and in Gaelic it is known as *coll*, the ninth letter of the Ogham alphabet. The Celts valued the nuts as symbols of poetry, love, childbirth and, above all, knowledge. Eating hazelnuts was considered the quickest way to navigate from naivety to knowing. Most famous of all mythological hazels were the nine trees growing around Connla's Well (the well of knowledge). As the nuts dropped into the water, their knowledge flowed into the spring.

Here the salmon absorbed the wisdom, showing a spot on their scales for each of the hazelnuts they had consumed. Only the god Nechtan, the 'bearer of knowledge', and his three cup-bearers were allowed to visit Connla's Well. So when Sinann (Shannon), granddaughter to Lir (god of the sea), tried to retrieve wisdom from it, the enchanted drowned her. Her body was washed up on the bank and the waterway was named after her – the River Shannon.

In 'The Boyhood Deeds of Fionn', a poet named Finn Eces and his pupil, Fionn, spent seven years trying to catch the elusive 'salmon of wisdom' (*An Bradán Feasa*). When they finally caught it, Finn told Fionn to cook it without tasting any of it. Fionn was following instructions carefully when a single drop of knowledge-imbued oil spat out of the pan on to his thumb, which he instinctively stuck into his mouth to salve the burn. When Finn saw his student, he could see from the look in his eye that Fionn had acquired the magical hazel's knowledge, and so instructed him to eat the rest. Fionn gained profound wisdom that he could amplify at will by biting the scar on his thumb. He went on to become one of Irish mythology's greatest heroes, Fionn mac Cumhaill, leader of the Fianna.

- Hazelnuts were the popcorn of Elizabethan England, and the Globe Theatre's floor in London was frequently peppered with their hard shells.
- In Old English tradition, 29 September was known as Crack-Nut Sunday, when the congregation could bring their hazelnut hoards to the Sunday service and crack them while the priest gave an (almost inaudible) sermon.
- In Ireland, a conjoined pair of hazelnuts was known as a *Cnò-chomblaich*, and these were sought-after charms against witchcraft and toothache.

CRATAEGUS MONOGYNA

COMMON HAWTHORN

The common hawthorn, also called whitethorn or May tree, is significant in both pagan and Christian traditions, as well as being associated with fairy folklore and popular superstition. In Celtic myth, the veil between the fairy and mortal worlds is thinnest at two points of the year: Beltane, when hawthorn flowers; and Samhain, when it fruits. At Beltane (or May Day) celebrations, the blossom features prominently. It heralds the arrival of summer, thus the idiom, 'Ne'er cast a clout till May be out' – in other words, do not put your winter clothes away until the hawthorn flowers.

In Glastonbury, Somerset in England, there is a unique *Crataegus monogyna* variant that flowers twice a year, in springtime and at Christmas time. The legend of the twice-blooming Glastonbury/Holy thorn started with Jesus's disciple, Joseph of Arimathea. After Jesus's crucifixion in the Bible, Joseph is said to have travelled to England with his hawthorn pilgrim staff and the Holy Grail, bringing Christianity to a local King Ethelbert and his people. At Glastonbury, Joseph reportedly hid the Holy Grail in the Chalice Well and planted his pilgrim's staff atop Wearyall Hill. Overnight, the staff grew into a biannual, flowering thorn tree, echoing Jesus's crown of thorns and the resurrection. Joseph is accredited with building Britain's first church on the spot that Glastonbury Abbey stands today, complete with a stained-glass window commemorating him and his hawthorn staff.

The tree was a popular pilgrimage until future Lord Protector of England Oliver Cromwell's Puritan soldiers chopped down the 'relic of superstition' during the English Civil War. The tree got its revenge on one soldier, who was supposedly blinded by a thorn while striking the tree with an axe. Monks discreetly took cuttings of the original tree to propagate, keeping the lineage alive until a second tree was planted. By the eighteenth century, local entrepreneurs were profiting from the miracle tree and today many signs still promote the sale of the original holy thorn in the town.

Whitethorn, a symbol of fertility in pagan traditions, has ancient links to Beltane, Calan Mai and other May Day celebrations to mark the start of summer.

Across Ireland, Scotland and the Isle of Man, the trees at Celtic holy wells (clootie wells) were decorated during Beltane festivities. The sacred sites are still destinations for pilgrims, who leave votive offerings and hang ribbons from the branches, hoping to be blessed with relief from an ailment.

Songs and dances were performed around the trunk of the 'May Bough', sometimes referred to as the maypole. Traditionally, the pole was a symbol of masculinity, and the ribbons femininity. Garlands of flowers were worn by the young women hoping to turn heads.

May Day processions are led by the Jack-o'-the-Green, a wicker-shelled figure, covered head to toe in foliage, with hawthorn among the mix. He is an expression of the Green Man, whose bushy face is often assembled from hawthorn leaves and acorns. The pagan festival, known for its strong sexual connotations, has prevailed despite efforts to extinguish it. It was banned by Oliver Cromwell in 1645 during the English Civil War (Cromwell appeared to have a particular disdain for hawthorn) but when the monarchy was restored in 1660 King Charles II ended the ban and erected a 40m- (131ft-) maypole in London. In Victorian times, pride in local Beltane trees was so strong that tree theft was not uncommon, leading to a 'May bush' ban.

Hawthorn also has a dark side. There is a widespread taboo that bringing hawthorn into your house will invite death and illness. Sleeping in a room with a blossoming cutting might be the last thing you do. These morbid superstitions may have stemmed from the observation that the sweet and heavy fragrance of the blooms was reminiscent of death and plague. More recently, botanists have discovered that the floral displays emit a chemical called trimethylamine, one of the first formed in decaying animals.

In Ireland, a solitary hawthorn bush is a perfect trysting site for fairies, so the trees must only be cut for medicinal or ceremonious purposes. Take heed lest you be snagged by a thorn and die of the infection.

In 1968, a proposed road in Donegal, Eire was rerouted to avoid a solitary hawthorn. Again, in 1999 the M18 expansion in County Claire, Eire came under heavy scrutiny after Irish folklorist Eddie Lenihan expressed his concerns in the *Irish Times* and *The New York Times*. Lenihan forewarned there would be a significant increase in fatalities on that stretch of motorway if they felled the tree. Remarkably, his advice was heeded and the motorway was rerouted at great expense. The tree, known as the Latoon fairy bush, is now visible from the road and drivers have reported seeing white fairy blood and gory remains left from fairy wars on it.

CUPRESSUS SEMPERVIRENS

MEDITERRANEAN CYPRESS

Fragrant, evergreen and conical, Mediterranean cypresses are heroes of the skyline. These trees have provided inspiration for many writers and artists, including Vincent van Gogh, who was devoted to the tree. He painted them bursting with life and energy, dancing like well-fed flames.

The trees are found on every continent apart from Antarctica; an impressive spread that is a result of species' longevity. Cypress fossils can be dated to the Mesozoic Era, a time when Earth was one giant continent. Later, when the tectonic plates broke the land mass apart, the trees followed, growing alongside the rise of early civilizations.

The ancient Persians venerated the tree in general, and in particular the now 4,500-year-old Cypress of Abarkuh. Believed to be the oldest living matter in Asia, this tree is visited by wish-makers who tie ribbons on its branches. According to some, it was planted by Japheth, Noah's son in the Bible, after the Great Flood. Others claim it was the prophet Zarathustra, founder of Zoroastrianism, who planted it. He believed that the evergreen tree symbolized Ameretat, the divine entity of immortality.

On another occasion, according to the Persian epic poem *Shahnameh*, Zarathustra took a branch of cypress from Paradise and planted it at the first Zoroastrian *agiary* (fire temple) in Kashmar. It grew old and magnificent, and became a symbol of the flourishing faith.

News of the Cypress of Kashmar spread far; in 861 CE the Abbasid caliph (al-Mutawakkil) wanted to see it himself but, unwilling to leave Baghdad, insisted it was cut down in pieces and reassembled at his palace. Despite protests by the people of Kashmar, it began its journey east on the backs of 1,300 camels. However, before the tree arrived, the caliph was assassinated at the order of his son, upholding the superstition that terrible misfortune would befall anyone who cuts down a cypress.

Following the Muslim invasion of Persia in the seventh century CE, the country's main religion switched from Zoroastrianism to Islam, but the idea of the cypress as the tree of immortality continued. Poets such as Shirazi and Rumi harnessed the tree's symbolism and beauty in their epics. It was planted in cemeteries and ornamental gardens, and depicted in artwork and literature, its image carved into tombs, painted in palaces and woven into Persian rugs.

Throughout history, cypress wood has been carved and scraped into many uses. Some of the earliest recorded idols from the Archaic Greece period (around 800 to 480 BCE) were chiselled cypress statuettes known as *xoana*. It is thought they may have been bathed and decorated to reflect their gods, carried in processions and worshipped in temples.

One, known as the Palladium of Troy, was sculpted in the image of Athena and said to have been dropped to Earth by Zeus himself. It was imbued with the magical power to protect the Trojan citadel from capture by the Greeks for as long as it stayed within the walls. It was the theft of the *xoana* that set the downfall of Troy in motion.

According to the ancient Greek philosopher Strabo, Leto gave birth to the divine twins Apollo and Artemis in a cypress grove, but the associations did not stop there. Temples in Artemis's name often adjoined sacred groves and the tree was used to represent her affinity to animals and plants. For Apollo, his connection to the cypress was forged in the story of Cyparissus, whom the god took as his mortal lover. The boy was devoted to a great bejewelled stag with golden antlers. It was his most beloved companion, but tragedy struck one summer's day when Cyparissus accidentally struck and killed the stag while practising with his javelin. The boy was so overcome with grief that he asked Apollo to turn him into a cypress tree so that he might mourn forever.

In both ancient Greece and Rome, cypress was referred to as the 'mournful tree'. The trees were planted near the dead, their branches used to build coffins and fuel funeral pyres, burning with a fresh, woody fragrance. There is one specimen, though, that has defied this association. Nestled in the cloister of a church in Verucchio, northern Italy, the tree is said to have been planted by the Catholic St Francis when he founded the convent in 1213. In the legend, St Francis threw his staff on the fire in a bid for warmth and was surprised to find it still lying among the ash the next morning, green and unburnt. 'If you won't burn, grow!' he exclaimed, and dug the stick into the earth. Cypress branches are capable of rooting in soil, and so it did and the tree still grows there today.

♦ A cypress design you might find in your home is the paisley pattern, named after a Scottish weaving town. It is said that its Persian 'boteh' motif, a symbol of fertility in the shape of a teardrop, represents a cypress tree bending under the weight of a songbird.

♦ Wood from the sacred cypress groves was relied upon in the framework for greater statues. Cypress is believed to have been used in the construction of the Athena Parthenos in Athens.

DRACAENA CINNABARI

DRAGON BLOOD TREE

Socotra, home to the dragon blood tree, is an otherworldly Yemeni island east of the Horn of Africa, in an archipelago that is making a slow pilgrimage across the Indian Ocean. It is one of the most isolated non-volcanic landforms on the planet, and is heaving with endemic fauna and flora, including the dragon blood tree, which erupts defiantly from Socotra's rocky surface. Silhouettes loom out of the island's morning mist and, as it recedes, serpent-like branches emerge, reminiscent of the multi-headed dragon Ladon from Greek myth. The tree's outwardly forking, twisted branches and blood-like sap may look like something from a fairy tale, but they are in fact a consequence of their unique habitat. The ferocious heat from the sun scorches the ground and makes water scarce. To combat this, the tree has developed a technique called 'horizontal precipitation capture'. Capitalizing on the occasional mists, it collects the humidity as droplets on its long, waxy, skyward-probing leaves. Funnelled down through the leaves in the mushroom-shaped canopy, droplets are encouraged further along the spongy branches. Some water is absorbed as it runs down, while the rest converges at the trunk, finally reaching the soil. The dense shade below affords a small chance for groundwater to be absorbed before evaporating, and protects the shallow roots from the blazing heat. Locking water into the system benefits not just the tree but also the surrounding ecosystem.

For thousands of years, the island of Socotra has been in the middle of an important trade route between India, West Asia, the Mediterranean and East Africa, and a welcome stop in miles of open sea. Its shores have played host to a cultural melting pot of visitors seeking shade and rest. The exchange of stories is perhaps the reason for the dragon blood's rich and varied mythology, spanning many faiths and languages.

The tree is known locally in Arabic as *Dam al-Akhawain* (the blood of the two brothers). These troubled siblings, Darsah and Samhah (named for two nearby islands), fought each other to death – their blood pooled in the coarse sand under their feet, and the trees emerged. Another origin story speaks of a dragon and an elephant. The dragon wrapped himself around the elephant, strangling him before drinking the elephant's lifeblood. As the elephant succumbed, he fell sideways, crushing the dragon. The blood of the two animals flowed together and in the pools of blood, seedlings grew. This story is mirrored in Hindu mythology and Roman literature alike. In the Hindu version, it is believed that the dragon represents Brahma and the elephant Shiva (gods of creation and destruction, respectively).

The narrative that these trees first grew from spilt blood is echoed in Greek myth. Legend has it that in ancient Greece, the many-headed serpentine monster Ladon coiled himself around a sacred golden apple tree in the gardens of Hesperides. His heads, each fitted with razor-sharp teeth, reared up in the canopy of the tree, guarding the bounty. The penultimate labour of Hercules was to retrieve the apples from the tree, and in doing so he slayed the dragon. Where Ladon's blood spilt, the tree grew (*see* APPLE, p. 85). To commemorate the serpent-like dragon's service to the gods, Ladon was painted in the night sky as the constellation Draco.

It is possible that the Greek version of this myth referred to the very closely related *Dracaena draco*, found not on Socotra but native to Macaronesia (off the coast of Europe and North Africa) and Morocco. The two species have much in common, including cultural prominence in their respective homes. Far from the Yemeni archipelago, on the island of Tenerife, there once stood a particularly noteworthy example of the *Dracaena draco* – the Great Dragon Tree. This colossus lived a long and interesting life. Once revered by the Guanches – the Indigenous people of the Canary Islands – it was a place of worship and ritual. In its shade, incoming leaders were crowned, but not before kissing the bones of their predecessors. It later became a place of pilgrimage for local peasants, who believed the tree could predict the coming year's weather, depending on which side blossomed first. In its final years, it was incorporated into the ornamental Franchy Gardens for the pleasure of visitors. One of these, German naturalist, explorer and polymath Alexander von Humboldt, took an interest in the tree, and amidst his documents is the claim that it was 6,000 years old. While this was likely an adventurous estimate, the slow-growing monster may have exceeded its thousandth birthday, ten years for every head, perhaps. But all monsters are slain in the end and not long after von Humboldt's visit, a fierce hurricane almost snapped off the giant's crown and it died shortly thereafter.

♦ When cut, the tree bleeds rich vermillion beads of sap, at one time believed to be authentic dragons' blood.
♦ The sap, known to be rich in antimicrobial and anti-inflammatory properties, was historically used by the Socotrans as a 'cure all', and known around the world as a 'liquid bandage'.

EUCALYPTUS

EUCALYPTUS

It is quite hard to capture the folklore of eucalyptus in writing, not because of a lack of it but because of the sacred manner in which the stories have been passed down. Traditionally, they could only be told by a few within the Aboriginal Australian community, and are carefully guarded.

The Europeans, who arrived in the eighteenth century, gave eucalyptus its common name, 'gum tree', on account of the tannin-rich exudate that seeps from its bark (*kino*). The gum tree comes in all manner of shapes and sizes, from small shrubs to giants reaching for the heavens.

To this day, eucalyptus wood is used to make ceremonial instruments such as clapping sticks, while termite-hollowed branches become didgeridoos. Its tremendous reach, versatility as remedies and importance in spiritual cleansing, ceremonies and storytelling have rooted the gums firmly into the lives of Aboriginal Australian communities. Some large gums, known as corroboree trees, are especially revered. They serve as meeting points for ceremonies where people gather to paint their bodies, dance, sing and perform Dreamtime stories. Outsiders are usually forbidden from attending and the stories are passed orally through generations in as many as 500 territorially anchored groups and 300 languages.

The ceremonies often begin with a cleansing ritual. Smoking bundles of leaves, carried on hot coals in a portable tarnuk (the hollowed-out burl of a eucalyptus tree) are wafted at the attendees. This ritual encourages good health and helps to identify and ward away bad spirits.

After the cleansing comes the main part of the ceremony, the result of which is the bora rings that are found in southeastern Australia, often in clearings of eucalyptus and other trees, consisting of two concentric circles on the ground. The earth has sometimes been so compacted and hardened by ceremony and dance here that old sites where grass is unable to grow are still visible. Surrounding old bora rings, you can often find 'scarred trees' – eucalyptus with sections of bark stripped away to reveal the heartwood. The bark was used for canoes and shields, while the heartwood was carved with intricate arborglyphs (symbols and shapes), marking sacred ceremony sites. The bark of the eucalyptus can also be flattened and is still used as a canvas for depicting Dreamtime stories. Bark paintings are now very valuable and sold worldwide, but storytellers still keep some subjects secret within their communities.

The bora ring circles are thought to symbolize the Milky Way or 'sky bora'. Some Aboriginal Australian communities believe the Milky Way is a giant, luscious creek in the sky, with a stream, ponds, reeds and eucalyptus all distinguishable in the stars – the sky country. In some accounts, this heavenly plain is propped up by eucalyptus poles, and both ancestral knowledge and an abundance of animals and plants can be obtained there. A popular theme across Aboriginal cultures is that tall trees can act as ladders between the Earth and sky landscapes. Some medicine men were said to gain new knowledge by climbing eucalyptus trees and learning from their ancestral spirits. In the stories of the Alawa people of Australia's Northern Territory, two ancestors climbed into the sky country on a large northern stringybark *Eucalyptus tetrodonta*. Since that day, they could be seen as stars in the

Pleiades constellation. Aboriginal Australians were among the world's first astronomers, with some community elders able to name almost all of the 3,000 stars in the visible sky.

One of the most accessible and widely shared Dreamtime stories is of a young orphan named Koobor. Koobor's cruel aunt and uncle hid their water from him whenever they left home. One day, they departed in haste and left the water out. The boy enjoyed a long drink, but feared what they would do on their return. Koobor hung the buckets on a branch of a eucalyptus tree and started to climb, singing an ancient song as he went. To his great surprise, he and the buckets started to lift higher and higher above the ground. When his aunt and uncle returned, they persuaded their nephew to come down, speaking softly and apologizing for the way they had treated him. Beguiled, the boy obeyed, but at the bottom he found no compassion, only a beating. Left with broken bones, the boy started to transform, growing fur and claws, before racing up to the top of the tree with remarkable agility. The koala-boy could survive solely on eucalyptus leaves, which are toxic to humans, and no longer needed his aunt and uncle's water.

- According to the Aboriginal Australian Dhirari people, large creatures called Kadimarkara once climbed down from the sky on huge eucalyptus trees. This legend was likely an attempt to explain the megafauna fossils they had found at Lake Eyre.
- Eucalyptus trees can live for over 1,000 years. When their hardwood rots away and large cavities open, they are known as 'birthing trees' – a safe and sacred place for pregnant women to deliver their babies.
- In the Arnhem Land, Northern Territory, Australia, hollowed-out logs of eucalyptus trees, called 'larrakitj', are decorated and used as an ossuaries to hold the bones and personal belongings of the dead.

FICUS BENGHALENSIS AND FICUS AUREA

BANYAN FIG AND STRANGLER FIG

Every species of fig tree has its own specialized wasp tasked with germinating the fruit. With this as their common feature, 'fig' (*Ficus*) describes a surprisingly diverse group of trees, from the fruit-bearing tree beloved by the Romans to the sinister-sounding 'strangler figs' – banyan being the most widely recognized. These types of fig trees have deep connections with Hindu and Buddhist mythology.

After the parasitic seeds of strangler figs are dropped on to a host tree (or ancient ruins, such as at Angkor Wat in Cambodia), root anchors are dropped to the ground as branches envelop and eventually kill their host. Often all that is left is an eerie hollow where malevolent beings can lurk. In the Philippines Gremlin-like *duwendes* and centaur-like *tikbalang*, notorious troublemakers both, protect the tree. In Australia a red, frog-like vampire known as the *Yara-ma-yha-who* might drop from the canopy on to unwitting passers-by to drink their blood through its hand and foot suckers. And in the hollow stranglers of Japan's Okinawa prefecture dwell extremely mischievous wood spirits known as *kijimuna*.

In a Vietnamese legend, Chú Cuội discovered a banyan's (*Ficus benghalensis* – illustrated) healing powers when he witnessed it reviving a tiger cub. He used the tree to heal a blind man and save a dying princess, whom he later married. He moved the tree to the palace garden and tended to it obsessively, neglecting his wife, who became envious and urinated on the tree. The disgusted tree ripped itself from the ground and started to fly away, but Cuội managed to cling to a root as it flew all the way to the moon. Traditionally, Vietnamese children light lanterns to try and help guide Cuội back home.

The peepul tree (*Ficus religiosa*) – also known as the sacred bodhi tree – represents knowledge and enlightenment, and is often found in the Buddhist and Hindu temples and shrines of southeastern Asia. They are so associated with worship that a 'visit to the peepul tree' has become a euphemism for prayer. Around 500 BCE, Siddhartha, who became known as the Buddha, is said to have reached enlightenment on his forty-ninth day of meditation under the sacred bodhi tree in India. The original tree was unfortunately poisoned but in 1881, the British Army engineer, Alexander Cunningham, planted a cutting of what is believed to be a descendant of the tree on the same spot, and nowadays many Buddhists make pilgrimage there.

The Kutia Kondh, an Indigenous tribal people on India's east coast, believe that when Goddess Nirantali created the world, she carried a handful of banyan seeds wrapped in leaves. After she created the sun, she planted the seeds so the trees would offer their shade to the people. The trees did not produce enough, so she stretched the leaves and pulled the branches to the ground.

As a Hindu symbol of life and connection between all human beings, the banyan represents the Trimurti.

Vishnu is represented by the trunk, Brahma the roots and Shiva the leaves. Hindu mythology tells that after the great deluge, Lord Vishnu's avatar Krishna was found floating on a leaf under a banyan tree, in the form of a small boy. A sage, who had watched the floods and dissolution of Earth as part of *pralaya* (the Hindu cycle of creation and destruction), noticed the infant was cradling the world and all its realms inside him, so he could release it safely back into the universe.

The banyan tree is also associated with Yama, the god of death, who was outwitted by Savitri in the Hindu epic of *Mahabharata*. When Savitri's husband Satyavan died under a banyan, she refused to let Yama take him. She outwitted the god and was rewarded with a wish. She asked for her husband to be returned to her and the two lived happily ever after. This legend inspired the Hindu festival of Vat Purnima (Festival of the Banyan), where women in western India celebrate their devotion to their husbands by tying a ceremonial ribbon around a tree.

There is a legendary, ancient tree named Thimmamma Marrimanu, near Andhra Pradesh, India, which holds the record for having the world's largest canopy, at roughly 2 hectares (5 acres). The stories tell that the tree started life when its recently widowed namesake performed *sati* (or *suttee*), throwing herself on her husband's funeral pyre. One of the sticks on the pyre took root in the couple's ashes and Thimmamma rose again, this time as a god and banyan tree. The tree is said to have powers of fertility and has become a pilgrimage for couples trying for a child.

- The Betsileo people from Madagascar believe damaging a banyan will bring bad fortune upon one's entire family.
- Some Oriyan tribes in India believe that damage of the banyan must be immediately remediated with the sacrifice of a goat.

FICUS CARICA

EDIBLE FIG

While many fig trees produce edible fruits, not all are palatable to humans. The juicy fig as we know it grows on only a minority of trees, making *Ficus carica*'s famed fruit a delicious exception. From the sycamore figs of the ancient Egyptians and the wild figs of the ancient Romans, to the tree present in the biblical Garden of Eden, fig trees have been valued across culture and religions for their shade, their fruit and their handy, loin-sized leaves.

In the Bible, the fig is the only tree in the Garden of Eden mentioned by name. After picking and eating the forbidden fruit, Adam and Eve's shame compelled them to cover their nether regions with the leaves of a *Ficus carica* tree. Given its proximity, the fig was often presented as the forbidden fruit itself, but over time the apple acquired this acclaim.

As described in the Gospel of Mark in the Bible, Jesus made an example of a fig tree when he found it in full leaf, but without fruit. He cursed the tree: 'May no one ever eat fruit from you again.' Soon thereafter, Jesus and his disciples returned to find it dead and withered on account of his curse. While the harsh treatment of the tree is somewhat uncharacteristic of Jesus with his goodwill to all living things, it was a parable for a lack of faith. The tree in leaf looked as though it should be fruiting, but as it was not, Jesus used it as a metaphor for the spiritually barren religious leaders and the Jews who did not accept him as a messiah, as well as an example of the power of faith – when Jesus asked God to kill the fig tree, He did. His disregard for the tree may also reflect the fig's close association with original sin in the Garden of Eden.

For ancient Egyptians, sycamore fig trees (*Ficus sycomorus*) were the only indigenous tree of substantial size that would grow in the climate, and only on the edge of the desert at that. In Egyptian myth, the sycamore fig is strongly connected with the sun. Trees on the eastern horizon were used as astrological markers to track the passing of the days. Fertility goddesses Nut, Hathor and Isis are known as the 'ladies of the sycamore'. The goddesses' association with the tree may stem from the connection between the fig fruit and the womb as a symbol of life, death and rebirth. Hathor emerged from the trees to welcome people to heaven. She was also said to give birth to the sun god Ra in its shade.

The closely related but unpalatable wild fig, known as the caprifig, plays a crucial role in the traditional pollination of the edible, cultivated fig. In a process called caprification, a wasp extracts pollen from the wild fig and transfers it to a nearby edible fig tree, allowing it to produce delicious fruits.

Ficus ruminalis was a sacred wild fig with a profound significance to ancient Rome. A large wild fig stood at the entrance to a cave known as the Lupercal at the foot of the Palatine Hill. Here was where a cradle holding twins Romulus and Remus was said to have washed ashore from the River Tiber and where a she-wolf suckled the boys as infants. As the brothers grew, so did their ambition to start a city along the river. But their shared dream was torn apart when they disagreed about the exact location of the city; a fierce fight broke out and Romulus killed Remus. Romulus would build the city above the tree and the cave, and name it Rome.

Later, rumours circulated that the moment Romulus's fig tree at the cave entrance died, a new tree sprouted spontaneously in the Roman forum. Considered a sign of the gods, it was believed that the fate of Rome was linked to the tree, its vitality of the utmost importance. The Roman feasts of Juno Caprotina – celebrating female slaves – were always held under the fig tree. They commemorated a handmaid who allowed herself to be taken hostage by the enemy before sneaking up a fig tree to raise a torch, a signal for the Romans to attack.

The ancient Greeks coveted the fig from the *Ficus carica* in a similar fashion to the olive. It was a delicacy and awarded at ceremonies as a symbol of honour. In Greek myth, during Titanomachy – a ten-year battle between the Olympic gods and their predecessors, the Titans – the Earth goddess Gaia turned her Titan son Syceus into a fig tree to evade the wrath of Zeus. This led to the formation of the Greek word *syko*. Subsequently, the word 'sycophant' is believed to have originated from the combination of *syko* and *phainein* meaning 'fig revealer', stemming from a time where there was an unpopular fig tax on merchants. 'Fig revealers' were self-serving opportunists who reported those avoiding the fig tax to the authorities in order to gain standing.

Today, a fig revealer could mean something else entirely. We are familiar with seeing ancient Greek and Roman sculptures adorned with fig leaves, but these modesty panels were a later addition as part of the Christian 'fig leaf campaign', reflecting the relatively modern association of nudity with shame. In the early fourteenth century, Michelangelo's *David* caused scandal among the Catholic clergy and sixty years after its creation, a fig leaf was placed over his genitals. It remained there until its removal in 1912, and now the leaf is an exhibit of its own at the Victoria and Albert Museum in London.

FRAXINUS
EXCELSIOR

ASH

For the Vikings, the ash was the tree of life or the world tree, and everything existed within it. Known as Yggdrasil, it encompassed all nine realms, including Niflheim (the underworld), Midgard (Earth), Asgard (the realm of the gods) and the day Yggdrasil shook, signalling the onset of Ragnarök (the world's end).

Yggdrasil had three huge roots that reached into three wells. The first well was Urdarbrunnr, representing destiny. The second was Hvergelmir, in the realm of the dead where Nidhogg, a serpent of immense strength and incalculable size, gnawed on the roots and fed upon the corpses of murderers. Finally, there was Mímisbrunnr, the wise giant Mímir's well of divine knowledge, for which Odin sacrificed an eye in order to drink from.

Much like wild ash trees, Yggdrasil supported a diverse range of flora and fauna. According to the *Prose Edda*, these include an eagle with knowledge of many things, a hawk called Veðrfölnir and a gossiping squirrel named Ratatosk, who provokes the eagle and the serpent with his slander. Four stags arch their necks to graze upon the tree's luscious leaves and the dew collects on their antlers, before flowing down to feed the world's rivers and replenish the three great wells. A goat called Heidrun also munches at the foliage of

Yggdrasil, nourishing her production of mead, which Odin uses to quench the thirst of the fallen and honoured warriors of Valhalla.

The Celts valued the protective, healing and strengthening properties of ash for wand-making, and their wizard deity Gwydion carried a magical ash staff that he used to conjure, among other things, a fleet of phantom ships. Later, Gwydion was reincarnated as an eagle perching in an ash tree. The Celts also believed that fairies made their homes in ash and that to damage an occupied tree would bring bad luck. On the other hand, it was also thought that ash could stop fairies and other malevolent beings from souring milk, and so churning staffs and pails were made out of its wood.

In Ireland, the towering Celtic deity Trefuilngid Treochair carried an ever-living stick laden with flowers, seeds and fruit, and where he shook it, sacred trees would grow, including the five 'guardian trees', three of which were ash, which rooted in the five provinces. Ash is also synonymous with the ancient Irish stick-and-ball sport of hurling, as it is used to make hurley sticks. The iconic sound of the hurleys colliding has inspired the idiom 'the clash of the ash'. For years, scores have been settled on the hurling pitch. In Celtic myth, an army of ancient magicians known as Tuatha Dé Danann were challenged to a game in 1272 BCE by the Fir Bolg people as they both sought control of Ireland. In the warm-up, the Fir Bolg won a bloody and fraught game, but the triumph was short-lived as they went on to lose the greater battle.

There are many equivocal folk rituals that claim to heal ailments using ash. For example, it was supposed that warts could be transferred from a person to an ash tree using a needle; pinning hair to an ash tree could get rid of whooping cough; and cows experiencing cramps might be relieved by placing a shrew in the plugged hole of an ash tree; as the shrew perishes, the cow recovers, it was said. In one English tradition originating in Hampshire, weak or injured children would walk naked through a manmade split in an ash tree. Efforts were then made to heal the tree and, if it recovered, so would the child.

If it is romance you were after, a sprig of ash under a pillow or in your shoe could help you to predict your future love matches. Or you could find an 'even ash' (a rare ash leaf missing the uppermost terminal leaflet, with an even number of remaining leaflets down each side), which is as lucky as a four-leaf clover. In Wales, groups of boys and girls would race to find such a leaf and the fastest pair would be a love match.

- Ash is one of the few woods that can be burnt green, as mentioned in the popular 1930s firewood poem by Celia Congreve, which states: 'ash green or ash brown is fit for a queen with a golden crown.'
- Vikings carried ash spears, leading Anglo-Saxons to call them *aescling* (men of ash).
- Ash is believed to have purifying effects on water and is often found growing beside Celtic holy wells in Ireland and the Isle of Man.

ILEX AQUIFOLIUM

HOLLY

Holly is famed for its prickly, glossy, evergreen foliage and striking red berries (botanically speaking: 'drupes'). Most famously festooning doors, puddings and mantelpieces at Christmas, holly was the star in pagan and Roman winter celebrations long before the arrival of the Christian festival.

The word 'holly' derives from an old English word *holegn*, meaning 'prickly'. Its Latin name refers to the completely unrelated, but also spikey-leafed tree, *Quercus ilex*, which is commonly known as the holm oak – 'holm' meaning, enjoyably, another old English word for holly.

It is not just etymological entanglement that binds the holly to the oak. Celtic folklore attributes the changing of the seasons to an age-old struggle between the mighty Oak King and his twin brother, the Holly King. Evenly matched in strength, the two find themselves locked in an endless tussle for the crown. Drawing power from their opposing solstices, the Oak King rules the summer, conceding to the Holly King during winter. This rivalry is a popular plot in mummers' plays and the Holly King was likely an inspiration for the Green Knight, Sir Gawain's foe in Arthurian legend.

During December celebrations of Saturnalia, the Romans festooned their homes with holly – a plant sacred to the god Saturn. During the festivities, wreaths or boughs were gifted between guests. The hedonistic merrymaking of Saturnalia was unique, as social dynamics were turned on their head.

Anyone in the house, master or slave, could be nominated 'Saturnalia King' and would therefore adopt the role of master of proceedings.

For the Romans, the holly tree's reputation was far-reaching. It was thought to ward off evil and symbolized abundance and renewal. Roman naturalist and author Pliny the Elder believed that as well as having multiple medicinal qualities, the flowers could turn water to ice and that throwing a holly branch towards an animal would cause it to lie down and submit. As fanciful as this sounds, holly's reputation for controlling animals inspired coachmen to fashion holly-wood whips until the eighteenth century.

The Celts also adorned their dwellings in holly during the darkest months. Depending how prickly or smooth a wreath was, the power dynamic of a household could sway to favour the husband or the wife. In Scottish folklore, a bough of holly above your door would prevent evil from entering. Druids brought bundles of holly inside their homes, inviting sylvan spirits to come and nest, offering mutual protection for man and fairy. But at the first sign of wilting, the holly would need to be burned and the woodland spirits freed. Should you forget, the fairies would lay waste to the coming year's crops. 'Burning the holly' later influenced the Christian Twelfth Night tradition of removing Christmas decorations by 6 January.

Initially, early Christians prohibited the use of holly as a festive decoration, and wreaths could only be hung outside the house, on the front door. However, slowly but surely, holly wove its way back into the Christian Christmas and new traditions emerged.

Known as the Holy tree or Christ's thorn, holly wreaths became a symbol of Jesus's crown that he wore during his crucifixion, the berries like drops of his blood. In one

Christian story, the baby Jesus was hidden from King Herod's men in a bush. As danger approached, the bush's leaves grew spiky to protect him. Jesus later thanked the holly by awarding it evergreen status.

In the popular carol, 'The Holly and the Ivy', the holly is said to represent Christ, and the ivy represents his mother – a symbol of fertility. This may hark back to an ancient winter solstice tradition, when the boys dressed in holly and the girls dressed in ivy, to then parade together.

In 1843, the popularity of Charles Dickens's *A Christmas Carol* redefined Christmas. The ghost of Christmas Present influenced the appearance of Father Christmas himself, while seemingly drawing influence from the Holly King: 'A jolly Giant, glorious to see' in a 'simple green robe, or mantle, bordered with white fur... on its head it wore no other covering than a holly wreath.'

In the winter months, holly's striking evergreen canopy and scarlet drupes punctuate rural hedgerows. Felling a holly was considered an ill omen, so farmers left them to grow out and made use of them as visual guides when ploughing their fields. George Campbell, the Eighth Duke of Argyll, was so in thrall of this superstition that he rerouted the plans for an entire road to avoid a single holly.

♦ In Britain, holly was thought to protect against lightning, and so was often planted near domestic dwellings to protect them.
♦ Holly was also said to prevent witches from running along the hedge-tops that they might otherwise use as a travel network.
♦ British tradition decrees that the sprig of holly atop a traditional Christmas pudding should be saved for the following year and placed under the new pudding to ensure the household's good fortune.

JUGLANS REGIA

WALNUT

The walnut is considered one of the first 'tree foods' known to humankind and was a species found in the ancient Hanging Gardens of Babylon. *Juglans regia* has tasty nuts, with hard, decorative timber and leaves that can be used in a range of treatments. The wrinkly, lobed kernels have an uncanny resemblance to the human brain and have therefore been used as treatment for mental illness, headaches, epilepsy and head injuries, according to the medieval Doctrine of Signatures, which ascribed therapeutic properties to plants based on their physical resemblance.

The trees are self-pollinating hermaphrodites and are able to continue to bear fruit under tough conditions. They have a tendency to leave the ground beneath their boughs leached and bare, due to a toxin they produce called juglone, especially potent in the black walnut *Juglans nigra*. These sheltered clearings have become a popular fictional meeting place for witches, demons and other unsavoury types.

There was one walnut tree that gained particular notoriety as a destination for witches. Centuries ago, along the banks of the Sabato river, at Benevento in Italy – the 'city of the witches' – there grew a legendary tree where all the witches of Europe would gather and dance around the tree. The Romans had built a temple of Isis (the Egyptian goddess of magic) in Benevento and the subsequent

Lombards likely continued to invoke the deity in their own pagan rituals. According to legend, seventh-century mounted warriors would hang goats and snakes from the walnut tree to joust at, hoping to acquire their strength by magic. The rituals would last several days, the Lombards revelling in fire, wine, women and music. Needless to say, it proved incompatible with the arrival of Christianity and the tree was uprooted by Bishop Barbatus. Apparently the devil fled from the roots in snake-form as it fell.

However, this was not enough to shake Benevento's association with witchcraft. The demonic gatherings continued, and where the old tree stood a new one appeared. Its stubborn resurgence only served to strengthen the bond between walnut trees and witch lore. The Benevento walnut tree's reputation for witchcraft and evil are still linked in the Italian language, as *noce* (walnut) and *nocere* (harm) share an etymological root.

Nocino (witches' liqueur) is a popular Italian walnut liquor with ancient Celtic origins. According to folklore, it was first made by witches on St John's Eve (also known as Midsummer's Eve) in June. For the best brew, the finest walnuts would be picked by barefoot virgins. Then the nuts would be left to collect the magical dew of St John's Eve before being infused into the alcoholic drink.

Since the walnut tree's shade harbours all sorts of evils, it is ill-advised to sleep beneath one, and if the roots creep into a nearby cattle shed, the cows are likely to become unwell. However, while the tree itself is feared as a dark and death-bringing presence, the nut enjoys associations with fecundity, fertility and faithfulness.

On the Christian festival Michaelmas Day, young Belgian ladies would turn to walnuts for marriage auguries. Prior to the day, some of the nut cases would be carefully opened, emptied and refastened. The girl who picked a complete nut, kernel and all, would soon be happily married.

In Greco-Roman myth, Apollo granted King Dion's three daughters the gift of prophecy, with the caveat that they must never intervene in matters of the gods. Later, Bacchus, the god of wine, visited King Dion and fell in love his daughter Carya, sleeping with her in secret. On his departure, his longing to return to Carya intensified, and this was prophesized by her two sisters Lyco and Orphe. When Bacchus returned, the sisters guarded Carya, breaking their promise to Apollo. Bacchus sent Lyco and Orphe fleeing into the mountains, where they were turned into stone. He immortalized Carya as a walnut tree, so that he and the other gods could remember her for eternity.

- In Italian tradition, carrying a three-lobed walnut in your pocket will protect against witchcraft, lightning and the evil eye.
- If you suspect a witch of casting a charm in Italy, a walnut under her seat will stop her from getting up.
- In Belgium, catching a black spider between two halves of a walnut shell and then wearing this as an amulet is supposed to alleviate a fever.

LAURUS NOBILIS

BAY LAUREL

Before the last Ice Age, humidity-loving laurel trees (also known as bay trees) covered great swathes of the world, but now they can mainly be found in pockets in the Mediterranean, where most of its mythology was formed. It was the go-to headwear for high-achieving Romans and is symbolic of victory and accomplishment to this day.

The laurel is the star of Ovid's most famous metamorphosis of all, in the story of Daphne and Apollo. Ovid's retelling in his narrative poem *Metamorphoses* begins in the aftermath of Apollo's heroic victory against a monstrous snake. Apollo, who shot the serpent with one hundred arrows, was boasting of his triumphs to Cupid, going as far as to mock the god of love's skill with the bow. Irritated, Cupid fired two arrows. The first struck the heart of Apollo and he became consumed with an insatiable lust for the nymph Daphne. The second arrow hit Daphne, filling her with a deep repulsion of Apollo. A game of cat and mouse began between god and nymph. When Daphne's strength was spent from the chase, she begged her father and the river god Peneus of Thessaly to transform her into a laurel. Her flesh became bark, her hair leaves and her arms branches – her feet rooted in the earth, and her face became the treetop. Yet even as a laurel tree, Apollo was drawn to her 'shining loveliness', kissing the bark and embracing the branches as if they were her limbs. Daphne, in tree form, recoiled, but Apollo's love knew no end.

He insisted that if she could not be his bride, she would at least be his tree. Whether it was Apollo's delusion or Daphne finally resigning herself, her canopy apparently nodded in consent. Apollo imbued the tree with eternal youth, making it evergreen so that the laurel would always 'wear the crowning glory of never-fading foliage'. Henceforth, Apollo wore a laurel wreath in devotion to his love and insisted, 'My hair, my lyre, my quivers will always display the laurel.'

The high priestess of the Temple of Apollo would burn branches of laurel, believing that the narcotic fumes would inspire visions and prophecies. Other priestesses would chew the stimulating leaves to bring forth divinations of their own. In honour of god and nymph, laurel wreaths were awarded to the victors of the sporting Pythian Games, which were dedicated to Apollo. In ancient Greece, the wreaths symbolized purity, with bloodied soldiers wearing them after battles to cleanse their souls from the horrors of war.

Over time, in ancient Rome, laurel (*laurus*) and laurel berries (*bacca lauri*) came to represent victory and accomplishment, and the wreaths were presented to high achievers in the military, sports and the arts. In fourteenth-century Renaissance Italy, the Latin term became popular once again and 'laureate' was used to celebrate distinguished poets. Throughout the seventeenth century, graduating students were crowned with wreaths of laurel berries. The term *baccalauréat* in French, anglicized to 'bachelor', is still awarded to those completing degrees. While the wreaths epitomize the pinnacle of success, a fall from grace is likely if you are complacent enough to rest on your laurels.

Julius Caesar was known to wear a laurel wreath in affirmation of his power and strength at the dawn of the Roman Empire, and Pliny tells a story about his heir, Augustus, involving the laurel in his *Historia Naturalis*.

Shortly after Augustus became engaged to Livia Drusilla, an eagle dropped a white hen in her lap while she was sitting in the garden. It carried a laurel sprig in its beak, symbolizing victory, peace, virtue and immortality. The future empress commemorated this auspicious event by planting a grove of laurels in the Prima Porta estate. From these trees were cut the wreaths that adorned a succession of Caesars and champions of Rome. Augustus's adopted son, Tiberius, is said to have hidden under his bed with a laurel wreath during a storm, believing it would ward off lightning. In the build-up to the suicide of the fifth emperor (and final emperor in the line of Augustus), Nero Caesar, it was said that the grove unaccountably wilted and died.

* When the fleet of Queen Elizabeth I of England survived the storm of the 1588 Armada (a naval attack by the Spanish) relatively unscathed, she commissioned the 'Dangers Averted' gold medal, depicting a bay tree on an island with the inscription 'Not even dangers affect it.'
* Across European folklore, laurel is said to protect against snakebites and act as a potent shield against witchcraft and the evil eye. It was also thought to repel the plague, with reports that people carried bay leaves in their mouth to protect themselves.
* The medieval European folk tradition of placing a laurel leaf under a pillow was said to evoke prophetic dreams – a handy trick for maidens seeking counsel on potential love matches. And when the choice was made, lovers who shared a snapped laurel twig would remain faithful.
* In English herbalist and botanist Nicholas Culpeper's 1653 *Complete Herbal*, he wrote of laurel, 'neither witch nor devil, thunder nor lightning, will hurt a man in the place where a bay-tree is.'

MALUS DOMESTICA

APPLE

The apple is a symbol of knowledge, immortality, lust and temptation. Without it we would not have had the Trojan War, Newton's convenient metaphor for gravity, the Beatles' record label or the temptation that caused Snow White untold amounts of hassle.

All cultivated apples have genetic origins in the wild crab apple (*Malus sieversii*) from the Tian Shan mountain range of Kazakhstan. Over time, stray pips took root along the Silk Road, eventually cross-pollinating with the European crab apple (*Malus sylvestris*). In Mesopotamia and ancient Greece the technique of grafting was introduced. This enabled cultivators to take a cutting from a pleasant-tasting apple and fuse it to rootstock of a smaller tree. The ancient Greeks then developed orchards, which came to Britain via the Romans.

The fact that the commonplace apple is both delicious and readily available can perhaps explain how it has become so intertwined with folklore. The Celts saw apples as a symbol of wisdom and immortality. Druids made wands from apple wood and burnt it in fertility rituals, and the enchanted island of Avalon, King Arthur's legendary resting place, translates from Breton as 'isle of apples'.

Avalon is not the only mythical garden to contain apple trees, of course. In the Bible's Garden of Eden, Eve gave way to temptation and picked the fruit from the tree of knowledge, urged on by a serpent, often interpreted as representing the devil. She shared the apple with Adam, but a lump got stuck in his throat, forming his 'Adams apple'. The Latin for apple, *malus*, translates as 'bad', referring to its connotations with original sin. And in the mythical Greek Garden of the Hesperides, Gaia presented Hera with a tree of golden apples to celebrate her marriage to Zeus. However, Hera feared the nymphs who cared for the garden would steal the fruit, and so enlisted the multi-headed dragon Ladon to guard the tree. Ladon was later slain by Hercules as he stole apples for his eleventh labour (*see* DRAGON BLOOD TREE, p. 53).

At the wedding of Peleus and Thetis, Eris (the Greek goddess of discord) placed a golden apple on the table of gifts labelled 'For the most beautiful'. The bitter dispute that broke out between Hera, Athena and Aphrodite triggered a domino effect that eventually led to the Trojan War. This is where the phrase 'Apple of discord', meaning the source of a conflict, originates.

In Norse mythology, Loki lured Iðunn and her box of magical apples out of Asgard, baiting her with the promise of fruits to rival her own. While Iðunn was missing, the gods aged rapidly, forcing Loki to retrieve her. On her return the gods ate her magical apples and their vitality was restored.

In the human realm, apples have long been associated with the ancient English tradition of wassailing, in which communities bless their orchards and rid the trees of unwanted demons to improve the coming yield. A wassail king and queen address the oldest tree in an orchard, waking it up by banging pots and shooting shotguns into the branches. The commotion is designed to scare away any evil spirits. Cider-soaked bread is then left for the birds and the previous year's cider is poured on the roots, to thank the tree.

Celebrations also include plenty of dancing, a performance by mummers (a theatrically disguised troupe of actors) and, of course, cider, which is usually mulled. There are many traditional wassailing songs, including this one originating from Somerset:

> There was an old man and he had an old cow
> And how for to keep her he didn't know how
> He built up a barn for to keep his cow warm
> And a drop or two of cider will do us no harm.

- ◆ The Cornish (south-west England) tradition of Allantide, celebrating the beginning of winter, sees friends exchanging polished red 'Allan apples', a token of good fortune. In a precarious game, apples with lit candles on top are hung from a wooden frame. Players must bite the apple without getting a face full of molten wax.
- ◆ In Dorset, England, Lazy Laurence is said to protect the orchard and its bounty of cider-making apples. He is known to make people fall asleep under the trees, disorientating them and giving them stomach cramps. (What else could possibly account for such symptoms?) When peasants displayed the same symptoms, it was said they had a 'touch of Laurence'.
- ◆ In Yorkshire, England, there is a sprite called Auld Goggie who guards the apples until they are ripe. Goggie would take the form of a giant caterpillar and would eat any children trying to steal the apples.

MANGIFERA INDICA

MANGO

For Hindus, the sweet, juicy mango is the food of the gods and has strong associations with prosperity, knowledge and love. It is also strongly associated with Siddhartha in Buddhism and the goddess Ambika in Jainism. In Hindu mythology, a mango flower placed on the tip of one of Kamadeva's arrows (the Vedic Cupid) represented one of the five aspects of love and desire.

In *Shakuntala*, the Sanskrit play by Kalidasa, the heroine utilizes a mango stick as an arrow, offering it to Kamadeva, to represent her longing for King Dushyanta. At the start of the play, our heroine is enthralled by a jasmine vine that clings to a mango tree, a natural union symbolic of her readiness for a relationship of her own. When she falls in love with King Dushyanta, the mango represents the blossoming love between them: 'Jasmine shows her youth in her fresh flowers, and the mango-tree shows his strength in his ripening fruit.'

Mango is sometimes referred to as the Jnana palam (the fruit of wisdom). The prized fruit plays a central role in a mythical race between Ganesha and his brother Murugan, who lived with their parents Lord Shiva and Goddess Parvati in the Himalayas. One day, the sage Narada came to visit and offered Shiva and Parvati a mango that bestowed divine wisdom upon the eater. At first, the couple were delighted but Narada revealed that the mango could not be shared, and so they returned it. When Ganesha and Murugan heard about this, they squabbled and wrestled over the fruit. Shiva intervened, suggesting the dispute be settled with a race – the first to go three times around the world would win the mango. While elephantine Ganesha had an ill-suited mouse as his mount, his brother Murugan had a nimble peacock. Murugan sped around the planet three times, as fast as he could. Seeing no sign of his cumbersome brother on the way, he felt sure he would win, but when he returned he saw that Ganesha had already been given the mango. Ganesha, who knew he would not win the race, had instead circled his mother and father three times, claiming that they were his whole world. Clever Ganesha, the patron of intellectuals, is often portrayed holding this fruit of wisdom.

In another Hindu myth, the mango represents fertility. A rajah who was struggling to bear a child with either of his wives, asked a sage for advice. As the sage meditated upon the problem underneath a mango tree, a fruit fell upon his lap. He gave it to the rajah as a remedy, and the rajah divided it between his wives. It worked, but when the time came, the wives gave birth to half a baby each. The rajah banished the half-formed newborns from his palace. A demoness found them and joined them to make one 'perfect' boy, who grew up to be the powerful and evil King Jarâsandha of Magadha.

In 1868, British author Mary Frere transcribed twenty-four oral folk stories in *Old Deccan Days; or, Hindoo Fairy Legends, Current in Southern India.* The mango features prominently in a tale about Little Surya Bai, who had nothing and was raised by eagles in the absence of her lost mother, a milkwoman. However, the rajah, who was already married, fell deeply in love with her. The happy couple were married, but the rajah's first wife jealously drowned Surya in a water tank.

When all seemed lost, a golden sunflower grew from the tank. The grieving rajah found love anew with the flower that reminded him of Surya, but his first wife scorched the flower and tossed the ash into the jungle. From the ash, a young mango tree sprang up. It was so fast-growing and beautiful that it became the:

wonder of all the country around. At last, on its topmost bough, came one fair blossom; and the blossom fell, and the little mango grew rosier and rosier, and larger and larger, till so wonderful was it both for size and shape that people flocked from far and near only to look at it.

The single exquisite mango was reserved for the rajah, but one day, when an exhausted milkwoman fell asleep under the tree, the fruit shook itself free and fell into her pail. Back home, the milkwoman was delighted when the mango transformed into her long-lost daughter. The reunions did not end there – the rajah and Surya Bai found each other again, and the girl who started with nothing had everything and the evil first wife was locked in a tower for the rest of her days.

Mangos also appear frequently in Buddhist literature – in some accounts the Buddha himself is born beneath one. In the *Jātaka*, in the 539th of 547 past-life stories, Buddha tells of his life as King Mahājanaka and how the mango inspired him to renounce his royal lifestyle. One day, he saw a mango tree in the royal gardens 'all broken and despoiled by the rude crowds that sought its fruit.' Next to it there stood another mango tree barren of fruit, but nonetheless 'green and strong, its foliage waving in the air.' Disenchanted with the pressures and demands of royal life, he found the lifestyle of the barren tree preferable: 'That pair of trees my teachers were – from them my lesson did I gain.'

MORUS ALBA

WHITE MULBERRY

> With time and patience, the mulberry leaf becomes a silk gown.
>
> Chinese proverb

The mythical Fusang tree, or the 'the leaning mulberry tree', of China was said to be home to ten crows, each carrying their own sun. Every day their mother, the sun goddess Xihe, would take one crow on her sun chariot and fly it around the world. One day the crows grew restless and all decided to fly from the mulberry tree at once. The heat from the ten suns scorched the Earth and drew out monsters that began to prey on humanity. Despite the emperor's pleading, the sun crows would not return. Eventually, an archer named Hou Yi raised his magic bow and shot a single arrow that pierced nine of the birds. The one surviving crow and his sun hid in fear and the world lay in perpetual darkness. Finally, the crow was roused to answer a rooster, who screamed 'brother' as loud as he could. The crow and his sun flew out to meet the rooster, and has done so every morning since.

Back on the earthly plain, the leaves of the (real) white mulberry tree, *Morus alba*, are the favourite food of the silkworm *Bombyx mori* (domestic silk moth caterpillar). The pair's relationship has been carefully managed by humankind for as long as 6,000 years to produce silk. Starting as China's best-kept secret, the cultivation of silkworms or 'sericulture' has led to the silkworm being one of the only domesticated insects on the planet.

The impact of the tryptic relationship (mulberry, moth and human) has been pivotal in the advancements of humankind. The demand for silk led to the formation of the historical Silk Road for global trade, paving the way for the movement of many plant species around the world, along with the cultivation of the apple (*see* p. 85). Trees as important as this demand folklore, myth and legend.

One popular origin story for the discovery of silk tells that 2,700 years ago the Empress Leizu was sitting beneath a mulberry tree drinking tea, when a perfect, white cocoon fell from above, landing in her cup. She marvelled as the cocoon began to unravel and offered out fine beautiful threads. The cocoon continued to uncoil until it filled her entire garden. The empress had just stumbled upon the secret of silk, putting her in the running alongside Newton for the best discovery made under a tree.

As demand for the lustrous fabric grew, China monopolized the industry, keeping the secrets of its production safe. However, around 500 CE, the secret of sericulture had found a way out of the country.

One legend said that on becoming betrothed, the King of Khotan told the imperial Princess of China that if she wished to continue wearing silk, she would have to bring the means for its production with her to his kingdom. In a sixth- to eighth-century painted votive panel, the princess is depicted smuggling mulberry seeds and caterpillar eggs in her headdress, to evade detection at the Chinese border. Also present is a four-armed representation of the God of Silk.

Another tale of two monks tells the story of how silk arrived in the Byzantine Empire in 552 CE. While carrying out missionary work along the Silk Road, the two monks were ordered by Emperor Justinian to retrieve the secrets of silk from Central Asia. Smuggling precious silkworm eggs inside bamboo tubes, they left China and made their way home. The eggs hatched on route, and the caterpillars timed it to perfection, producing their cocoons on cue as they were presented to the emperor in Constantinople.

The silk trade grew to be a huge industry in Europe. The Italian cities of Venice, Genoa, Florence and Milan, and the French city of Lyon, became heavyweights of the featherweight commodity. During the British Industrial Revolution, silk weaving was in high demand, but due to the cold climate, attempts to cultivate home-grown silkworms from the white mulberry were largely unsuccessful. Those hoping for success were left disappointed, and this is one theory behind the origins of the well-known rhyme.

> Here we go round the mulberry bush,
> The mulberry bush,
> The mulberry bush.
> Here we go round the mulberry bush
> On a cold and frosty morning.

Another theory has its roots in prison, about the 200-year-old mulberry tree that until recently grew in HMP Wakefield, West Yorkshire. A popular belief is that the rhyme was created by the female prisoners who, exercising around the tree to keep warm, made up the song to entertain their babies.

OLEA EUROPAEA

OLIVE

Like the apple, olive trees were initially cultivated from a wild variant, *Olea oleaster* (wild olive). Grown for its fruit, oil and timber for over 5,000 years, it is esteemed for both the treasure it provides and its value to history and myth.

The slow-growing olive twists and groans its way to a staggering old age. Ancient groves thrive away from conflict and pollution in pockets of calm and timeless existence. Representing life, sustenance and rejuvenation in Christianity, Judaism and Islam, the olive tree is a symbol of peace that spans faiths and secular cultures alike.

The sprigs and wreaths, potent with symbolism, appear in many great works of art, including portraits of Julius Caesar, Alexander the Great, Queen Elizabeth I, Oliver Cromwell and King Louis XV, to name a few. A 3,000-year-old olive leaf collar was even found in Tutankhamun's tomb. Picasso's dove of peace, carrying an olive sprig in its beak, became synonymous with the pursuit of peace after the Second World War.

Crete, the mythical birthplace of the goddess Athena, was among the first cultivators of the olive, as far back as the fourth millennia BCE. When Athena found herself in a tussle with Poseidon for the leadership of Greece's Attica region, Zeus proclaimed the citizens would choose, and so both gods were given the opportunity to present a gift. Athena planted an olive tree and Poseidon struck a stone with his trident to create a saltwater fountain. The citizens favoured the olive tree's endless bounty and chose their goddess, naming the city Athens. Every year, the city celebrated Athena during the festival of Panathenaea, hosting banquets, processions, athletics and music. The athletes, who performed naked and slick with olive oil, competed for a painted amphora filled with yet more olive oil from the sacred grove of Academe.

This grove, originally planted in Athena's honour, became the site for Plato's academy. Under the boughs, the great mathematician and philosopher tutored a young Aristotle, among other esteemed alumni. The academy and grove were later flattened by a Roman incursion in 86 BCE, but there was a single surviving tree, which re-emerged, phoenix-like, from its surviving rootstock. The tree was named Plato's Olive and was held with great reverence until its demise in 1976, when its downfall finally came, not at the hands of the Spartans or Romans, but at those of a local bus driver who crashed into it.

Olive-club wielding demi-god Hercules was saddened by the lack of trees surrounding his father's temple at the foot of Mount Olympus and so planted a grove. When he held the first Olympic Games to further honour his father, the grove offered shade to the fatigued athletes. In the subsequent games, Olympians would receive a wild olive wreath, to be replaced eventually by medals.

The works of Hesiod and Homer are peppered with references to the olive tree. Odysseus encountered the olive tree many times during his epic twenty-year quest, using its canopy for shade and stabbing Polyphemus's cyclops eye with a splinter of its wood, before finally returning to his wife Penelope and the marital bed fashioned from its roots.

The olive was equally important to the Romans. On their coins, Mars, the god of war and peace, was shown bearing an olive branch in one arm and a spear in the other.

Similar imagery is also found on the Great Seal of the United States, which shows an eagle carrying an olive branch in one talon and thirteen arrows in the other, demonstrating both ambitions of peace and readiness for war.

Established by the ancient Greeks and Romans as a symbol for peace, Christians added hope and salvation to the olive's associations. Most famously, when the biblical flood started to recede, Noah sent a dove to find land. When the bird returned carrying a freshly plucked olive leaf, he knew the waters had abated. If we were to follow the flight of Noah's dove, we might find ourselves in the mountain village of Bshaaleh in Lebanon. Here grow sixteen ancient olive trees. For 6,000 years, these 'sisters' rose above the biblical floods, endured harsh mountain weather, conflict and perhaps even saw a dove or two.

Another biblical olive tree grew in the Garden of Gethsemane, and was dubbed 'the tree of agony' after the shame of Judas's (disciple of Jesus) great betrayal. The olive grove, a favourite praying spot of Christ and his disciples, became the site of the arrest orchestrated by Judas and the Roman guard that consequently led to Jesus's crucifixion. The trees are said to have been felled in 70 CE, but the grove remains, possibly resurrected – Christ-like – from the original root system.

- Like the ancient Greeks, the Romans gorged on the olive's bounty, as shown by the ancient spoil heap of Monte dei Cocci, which is 1.6 km (1 mile) wide and made from thousands of amphora fragments.
- Roman naturalist Pliny the Elder wrote passionately about olive trees. In his most famous text *Natural History*, he criticizes the Greeks, 'those parents of all vices', for how they 'abused it by making it minister to luxury, and employing it commonly in the gymnasium.'

PHOENIX DACTYLIFERA

DATE PALM

This tree, associated with renewal and rebirth, grows with its feet in the water and its head on fire, as an old saying goes. Demanding temperatures in excess of 50°C (122°F), the nourishing fruits offer a lifeline in desert regions of West Asia. Sweet and sticky dates are a worldwide delicacy and the sap, date honey, was the 'drink of life' in ancient Egypt. Almost every part of the tree has a use.

'The Babylonian Tree' is one of the oldest surviving poems from the pre-Islamic Parthian language. In 120 verses it details an argument between a date palm and a goat about who has the greatest worth. One interpretation is that the goat portrays Parthians and the date palm the Mesopotamians. Unsurprisingly, the Parthian narrative sees the goat the victor.

After the first Muslim states were established in the seventh century CE, the earliest agricultural book written in Arabic, *The Nabataean Agriculture*, emerged. The origins are murky, but a more complete version was compiled by Ibn Waḥshīyah in the late ninth to early tenth century. Thanks to partial translation, this sometimes-controversial text gives us a glimpse at the date palm's early influence in early Islamic and Chaldean civilization.

The text describes the effects the moon had on the date palm and how the movement of the sap affected its productivity – a similar practice to lunar gardening today. In the book's 'index of importance', the date palm was categorized as superior to all other plants, being more useful than even the olive tree. It recounted how the tree possessed sensitive faculties, making it closer to human and animal than plant. Indeed humans and date palms were believed to be closely related.

In the book, a magician suggests that a talisman of honey-covered plates, etched with the image of a date palm or a human and buried by a tree, would bring health and large yields of sweet fruit.

There are also mentions of characters in the book who later appear in both the Qur'an and the Bible, though they are more like ghosts or parallels of their future manifestations. In this text, Adam was said to be the forefather of the Chaldeans, rather than the whole of humankind. He played many important roles, including naming everything, teaching mathematics and cultivating trees. The ever-useful date palm was named 'the sister of Adam', having multiple skills to offer humankind being considered a family trait.

The Qur'an also draws connections between Adam and the date palm: 'There is among the trees, one which is blessed – it is the date palm, for it was created from the earth left over from the creation of Adam.'

The date palm is mentioned twenty times in the Qur'an, more than any other fruit tree. The prophet Muhammad endorsed its purifying qualities, claiming in Volume 7, Book 65, Number 356: 'Whoever takes seven 'Ajwa dates in the morning will not be effected by magic or poison on that day.' It is still considered by many to be the best way to break the fast of Ramadan.

Likewise, the date palm features strongly in the Bible, clocking up more than fifty mentions. The most notable is in relation to Palm Sunday, the Christian celebration marking Jesus's triumphant entrance into Jerusalem. Days before his crucifixion (and a week before his resurrection) Jesus was welcomed by crowds waving palm fronds, now symbolically recreated with palm crosses to mark the occasion. For Christians, palm fronds were a symbol of martyrdom and overcoming sin and mortality.

Previously, in Archaic Greece palm had a particular association with the god Apollo, who was born in the shades of its fronds on the isle of Delos. Apollo's temple was built on the island and became the meeting point for a large confederacy that opposed the formidable Persian Empire. After their significant victories at the Battle of Eurymedon, the Athenian war strategist Cimon erected a bronze palm tree in commemoration. Subsequently, palm fronds became synonymous with victories throughout the Greek world. *Phoenix dactylifera* was also seen by the Greeks as representing the cycle of life and death. Every year the palm would drop its dead, lower fronds, only to replace them with lush new growth on its crown.

The tree's association with renewal and rebirth, and its plumage-like canopy, has inextricably linked it, in some regional Egyptian and Greek mythology, to the immortal phoenix bird. According to legend, after five centuries of life, the 'firebird' constructs a large nest in the palm's lifted canopy before succumbing to its famous fiery inferno. From the ashes there is born anew the next generation of phoenix – of which there can only ever be one at a time. (Other traditions link the phoenix with frankincense, *see* p. 25.)

PICEA ABIES

NORWAY SPRUCE

The Norway spruce has a double life: in the dark and in the light. While most grow peacefully in the shadowy, dense forests of northern Europe, many find themselves felled, dolled up and set to twinkle each year at Christmas time. It is in both the impenetrable gloom of the forest and the sparkling lights of Christmas that their folk tales are born.

The Norway spruce now makes up around half the trees in the mostly evergreen and densely packed Schwarzwald region of Germany, otherwise known as the Black Forest. Some claim it was the Romans who were the first to call it that (*silva nigra* in Latin), as they allegedly feared the darkness cast beneath the spruces' opaque canopy. In fact, at that time the forest would have contained a greater mix of trees, but the spruce would still have commanded great swathes in the higher altitudes and the darkness on the forest floor would have extended for miles.

One particularly chilling tale of the Black Forest concerns a malevolent fairy known as *Der Großmann* (the tall man), who had long, spindly arms and large, moon-like eyes in an otherwise featureless face. He would lure misbehaving children away from their homes, tapping at their window or trapping them in his tangle of arms, before chasing them into the oblivion of the woods.

It is perhaps surprising that a tree with such dark associations could become the original celebratory Christmas tree, but maybe the idea of bringing light to the darkest part of year makes it an apt choice. The custom probably originated with the Viking celebrations of *Jolablot* (Yule). On the winter solstice, the Vikings welcomed the sun's return by feasting, gift-giving, sacrifice and bringing in the yule log and the yule tree. The yule log, usually oak, would burn for days, and it was considered a very ill omen if it burnt out during the festivities. Then there was the yule tree – likely Norway spruce – whose evergreen branches represented eternal life and may have been decorated with treats and wooden Norse god figurines. It is said that one Viking would don a white beard and assume the role of 'old man winter', perhaps a reference to Odin.

The Germanic people continued their Yuletide celebrations in this manner for centuries before Christianity swept the country. Legend had it that on one Christmas Eve, St Boniface, known as the apostle to the Germans, (*c.* 675– 754 CE) interrupted a pagan sacrifice dedicated to the Norse god Thor that was taking place beneath an oak. The monk took an axe and felled the tree, and the pagans, disillusioned by Thor's failure to intervene, were in awe of the monk's strength. St Boniface pointed at a nearby spruce and declared it the true tree of God, representing eternal life. He compelled the pagans to bring this holy tree into their homes, elegantly putting a Christian spin on centuries of pagan tradition.

During the medieval era, a German Christmas tradition brought the spruce tree inside as part of the Catholic *Paradise Play*, performed on Christmas Eve. The play told the biblical story of Adam and Eve through to the birth of Jesus in Bethlehem. An essential prop, the spruce was adorned with apples to look like the tree of knowledge (*see* APPLE, p. 85).

The popularity of Christmas trees grew, and they became a familiar site in German squares and households, where they would be decorated with apples, chocolate and, later, candles. In the seventeenth century, in the mountain village of Lauscha, glass-blowers perfected the art of blowing glass into small orbs and the bauble was born. It soon became a favoured alternative to the apple.

Soon enough, the Christmas tree became a tradition across other parts of Europe. In Ukraine, a folk tale tells of an impoverished family who went to sleep on Christmas Eve with a bare tree. When they woke, they discovered with delight that the spiders of the household had decorated the tree with intricate webs, turning gold and silver in the sunlight – the first tinsel.

The Christmas tree did not appear in British culture until 1848, when the *Illustrated London News* featured the royals at Christmas time with illustrations of Queen Victoria, Prince Albert and their family around a decorated spruce imported from the German prince's hometown of Coburg. Shortly after, Charles Dickens released a short story told from the perspective of a spruce, reminiscing fondly of its past. Before long, the Christmas tree was on everybody's wish lists, especially among the upper classes.

Back in the wild, little red and white toadstools (fly agaric) grow underneath the Norway spruce (*see* SILVER BIRCH, p. 21), resembling colourful presents. During the midwinter festivals of Siberia, a shaman was said to harvest these toadstools before visiting the snow-covered yurts of the village. As the doors were buried beneath the snowline, the shaman gained entry through the smoke hole atop the tent. He would leave a gift for the residents at the hearth: a bag of the hallucinogenic fungi. Perhaps it is the mushroom's influence that gives us the account of the shaman's subsequent departure, carried off by reindeer into the starry night sky.

PINUS

PINE

Whether in plantations to provide fast-growing lumber or in the ancient forests that survive in pockets, the needled pine is stitched across much of Earth's surface. From the Caledonian forest in the Scottish Highlands, to the Ailao mountains in China, these evergreens capable of multi-millennial lifespans are associated with longevity, steadfastness and eternal life. The bristlecone pine, *Pinus longaeva*, can stand for over 5,000 years – longer than any other tree. Indeed, when the oldest living bristlecone was a sapling, the first Pharaohs of ancient Egypt were yet to build their pyramids. The Egyptian god Osiris carried an association with the pine: his staff was adorned with a pine cone that symbolized his eternal nature. Roman astrologer Julius Firmicus Maternus also recounted a worship ritual whereby an image of Osiris was sculpted from the wood of a felled and hollowed pine tree, then placed within the hollow before being ceremoniously burnt exactly a year later.

In the dramatic highlands of Scotland, where pines brave the exposed landscape, the trees were used as markers for the burial sites of great heroes and chieftains, as well as navigational markers for ancient crossroads and guides for weary drovers who might be seeking shelter for their livestock. The dramatic deforestation of this area was initiated by the Norse and the Celts, who over-harvested the trees for shipbuilding. An orally shared story from the Cairngorms mountain range goes that a visiting Nordic king envied all that the forest had to offer, coveting the pine wood for his ships and houses. However, when none of the forest animals would accept his rule, he became frustrated and planned to destroy the forest. One day, a pine marten overheard him speak of a monster who would help him – a monster whose single weakness was a silver arrow.

The monster, who happened to be his mother-in-law, appeared, with eaglelike wings, a whale-sized body and fiery breath that she sprayed over the trees. The king, who possessed dominion over the wind, billowed the flames south and laid waste to much of the forest. The pine marten sought a noble hunter to execute the monster, shooting the silver arrow through her eye. Her body fell to the forest floor, rotted, and the stench covered Scotland. A swarm of mysterious red and black insects descended on her corpse, stripping the flesh and eliminating her foul odour. The insects – ants – remained as caretakers of the forest.

Later, in British Arthurian legend Merlin was said to have acquired his magical powers in this same forest. During the Battle of Arfderydd, *c.* 573 CE, a bard named Myrddin Wyllt reportedly went mad and retreated into the trees. After fifty years of wandering, he returned as a wizard endowed with the gift of prophecy, and ultimately became King Arthur's esteemed advisor.

One solitary Scots pine on Doon Hill in Aberfoyle is said to contain the spirit of the seventeenth-century minister and folklorist Reverend Robert Kirk. In his most famous book, *The Secret Commonwealth of Elves, Fauns and Fairies*, he speculated that the tree was the gateway to the fairy realm. However, before the book was published, he was found dead on Doon Hill. The mysterious circumstances led to much speculation that his soul had been abducted by the fairies.

In both ancient Greece and Rome, the phallic shape of pine cones was associated with male fertility, vitality and strength. Dionysus/Bacchus, god of wine, festivity and fertility, carried a staff called *thyrsus* that was crafted from a rod of fennel and topped with a pine cone. *Pitys*, meaning pine in ancient Greek, was the name of a mountain nymph. She asked the gods to hide her from Pan's unwanted advances, so they transformed her into a pine tree. Pan also pursued a wood nymph named Syrinx, whom the gods disguised as reeds – the very same reeds that Pan cut and fashioned into his iconic panpipes.

In Japan, the evergreen pine is associated with a happy marriage, as told in one of the oldest Japanese stories 'The Takasago Legend'. Two pine spirits, Jō and Uba, reside within a pair of pine trees located in different towns. On moonlit nights, they meet in the spirit world and emerge together from a misty lake in Sumiyoshi to walk the Earth. While the two wander, enjoying each other's company, they clear fallen pine needles from the ground. The pair represent perfect harmony.

♦ The Trysting Pine on Barnham Cross Common, Norfolk, England, has a loop in its main trunk. If couples hold hands through the loop, kiss and pledge undying love, the tree is said to bind their devotion.
♦ Scattering a mix of male and female pine cones across a wedding table is considered a good omen for the happy couple.
♦ Pine cones are an example of the Fibonacci spiral in nature (or golden spiral), a shape derived from a series of numbers where each number is equal to the sum of the two numbers preceding it. The shape's eye-pleasing beauty also influenced the works of artists such as Leonardo da Vinci and Salvador Dalí.

POPULUS

POPLAR

The black poplar, *Populus nigra* (also known as 'ballerina poplar'), is the rarest native tree in Britain, famous for its iconic 'devil finger' red catkins. Once thriving in wetlands, it has fallen victim to habitat loss, over-exploitation and susceptibility to disease. Its isolation and a lack of female trees renders wind-born pollination ineffective. But John Constable's 1821 painting, *The Hay Wain*, is a quintessentially English reminder of how these beautiful trees once lined the riverways.

Perhaps it was the poplar's dramatic, dancing form that accounted for its popularity in ancient Greek and Roman myth. The Hamadryads, for example, were a group of wood nymphs of unequalled beauty who each formed a bond with a particular species of tree. Aigeiros was the nymph of the black poplar and Leuke was the nymph of the white poplar. Leuke was so admired by the god Hades/Pluto that he abducted her and took her to the underworld. After her death, Hades turned her into a white poplar tree in the Elysian Fields, which was an afterlife paradise for heroes and the virtuous.

For his tenth labour, the demi-god Hercules was asked to collect a herd of cattle that belonged to the monster Geryon, a three-headed, six-legged brute who had emerged from his mother Medusa's decapitated head. After slaying many beasts, including Geryon and Orthrus, Hercules had the taxing task of herding the cattle all the way back to Greece, but a bull named Italus broke free and swam to the nearest land, supposedly giving name to Italy. After vanquishing Cacus, a fire-breathing giant, Hercules returned triumphant. His victory was celebrated with the construction of an altar surrounded by white poplar trees that were consecrated in his name. Hercules and the men celebrated by weaving the leaves into each other's hair.

For his twelfth and final labour, Hercules subdued the three-headed dog Cerberus, using nothing but his raw and unimaginable strength. After doing so he constructed a crown made from the branches of Leuke's tree on the Elysian Fields. When the hero left the underworld with the Cerberus, it is said they were subjected to scorching temperatures that darkened the tops of the leaves while the undersides were protected by the hero's brow.

Crowns of *Populus tremula* – quaking aspen – are also said to grant safe passage into and out of the underworld, and can be found in European burial mounds, buried with the deceased. The word 'aspen' stems from the Greek *aspis*, meaning 'shield'. The Celts, who may have used poplar timber to fashion shields, also believed the tree had a connection with the living and the dead. They believed that the shimmering displays of the heavenly 'whispering aspen' canopies were communicating with the neighbouring world of the dead. Its association with communication extended further, with Highlanders believing a leaf placed under your tongue could make you more eloquent.

The USA has its own very similar native quaking aspen: *Populus tremuloides*. According to the Indigenous Ute tribe, when news spread that the Great Spirit was visiting, all the animals and plants trembled in anticipation of paying homage. All, that is, apart from the aspen, who was too beautiful and proud. The Great Spirit, in fury, decreed that as punishment the arrogant aspen would henceforth tremble when someone set their eyes upon it. Similarly, Indigenous Blackfoot tribe believed the tree's insolence to demigod and first man Na'pi when he walked past led to him beckoning a fury of lightning strikes down on the aspen trees, making them shake in fear forever more.

Christian tradition subverted the pagan reverence for *Populus tremula*, claiming it was the tree that made the crucifix (though many trees have been put forward for this). The belief led to the conclusion that the aspen's leaves quivered in shame at their associations with Christ's death. Christian, Greco-Roman, Native American or Celtic, the displays of an aspen are unanimously mesmerizing and, in reality, we have the leaf's extraordinarily long and delicate petioles (the stalk that attaches the leaf to the stem) to thank.

♦ The cultivated black poplar 'Lombardy', which is a familiar sight throughout northern Europe, was frequently planted by Napoleon along military roads to provide shade and navigation for his troops.
♦ Leonardo da Vinci's *Mona Lisa* is painted on a board of poplar.

PRUNUS SERRULATA

JAPANESE CHERRY

In the cherry blossom's shade
there's no such thing
as a stranger.

Kobayashi Issa

In Japan the cultural significance of the cherry tree is far-reaching, with daily televised blossom forecasts helping citizens time their trips to parks and arboretums. The tradition of picnicking underneath the blossom (*hanami*) stretches back hundreds of years. Initially, picnics were held under plum trees, but by the twelfth century the cherry tree took the limelight due to the dramatic inflorescence of its petals or *sakura*. During the eighteenth century, shogun Tokugawa Yoshimune planted cherry trees along vulnerable riverbanks, having the foresight that the blossom would attract large crowds, compact the earth and prevent erosion.

The relatively short lifespan of the tree itself and the brevity of the annual blossom display symbolizes life's impermanence and serves as an annual reminder to savour the present. There is life, death, beauty and violence in three short but glorious days. This reflects the lives of Japan's revered samurai, who live and die by the warrior code of *Bushido*, honouring their destined time to fall.

In Japan's two largest religions, Shintoism and Buddhism, the cherry tree is greatly valued. At the heart of most Shinto shrines are sacred trees, known as *shinboku* (god trees). There are many species that are venerated in this way – camphor, cedar and oak, among others – recognizable by the large, twisted ropes that ring the trunks. It is believed that these trees are home to *kami* (spirits) and, more specifically, *kodama* (tree-dwelling spirits). The Japanese cherry tree is a particularly popular arboreal conduit for the gods, spirits and souls of the dead and, as with all *shinboku*, it is shrouded in the superstition that mistreating one will bring great misfortune.

So revered are Japan's trees that they often become a character in the story themselves, with the soul of a person fusing with the tree and lending it the qualities they possessed in life. The story of the *Jiu-roku-zakura* tells of a very old samurai who watched with sadness as his family and friends died before him. All he had left was a beautiful old cherry tree that cradled the memories from his long life. The final blow came one day when he found the tree had died, leaving him bereft. On the sixteenth day of the year, the old samurai knelt down and said, 'Now deign, I beseech you, once more to bloom, because I am going to die in your stead,' before performing *hara-kiri* (a ritualistic suicide). As the samurai's ghost ascended, his life force entered the withered tree and within the hour it was decorated with fine blossom. The tree that used to flower in spring now flowered in winter on the sixteenth day of the year, surrounded by snow.

The tale of *Hanasaki Jiji* bestows the gift of bringing new life to the cherry tree on another. This time, the story goes, there once lived a kind elderly couple and their beloved dog. One day, the dog was digging in the garden and uncovered a pile of gold coins. Their envious neighbour, seeing their good fortune, asked to borrow the dog, but when he set it to work in his own garden, it found only mud and bones. The neighbour killed the dog and buried it under a nearby pine tree.

The kind old man noticed the pine tree grew at an unnaturally fast rate. He felled it and used the wood to make a new pestle and mortar. When he pounded barley in his new mortar, the grains multiplied and spilled out. Again, the neighbour saw, but when he borrowed the pestle and mortar, he received a meagre portion of insect-infested grain. Fuming, he threw the pestle and mortar into the fire.

That same night, the old man had a dream where his beloved dog showed him the whereabouts of a bare cherry tree. When he woke, the man took the ashes of his pestle and mortar, located the tree his dog directed him to in the dream, and scattered the ashes around the tree's trunk. Even though it was midwinter, the tree produced an incredible blossom, catching the attention of the local feudal lord. Amazed at the old man's accomplishment, the lord rewarded him with gifts. The jealous neighbour watched on and decided to scatter some ashes near another tree close by. But the ashes were caught by a gust of wind and blew into the unforgiving lord's eyes. The envious neighbour was seized and ousted from the town.

In Morioka, Japan there grows a national treasure known as the stone-splitting cherry tree. Beginning life as a tiny seed in a small crack, the 400-year-old tree appears to sit on top of a huge boulder, but in fact has cleaved the boulder neatly in half with perseverance, strength and resolve to survive. The tale goes that a humble stonecutter was in such awe of the *sakura* that he wished to become a cherry tree himself. Wish granted, the man's spirit was received by the tree and their personalities entwined, the mason's mastery of the rock allowing the tree to drive a split right through it.

PUNICA GRANATUM

POMEGRANATE

The pomegranate tree, with its showy flowers and iconic red fruit, has ancient associations with life and fertility. It is mentioned in the Old Testament of the Bible, the Qur'an, Talmud, and ancient Egyptian and classical literature. Its image adorns a Mesopotamian vase dating as far back as *c.* 3100 BCE that depicts Inanna, the goddess of love, sex and fertility. In Renaissance art, the baby Jesus is often depicted carrying a pomegranate as a sign of his passion and his sweetness, the juice representing the blood he sacrificed. In Buddhism, it is one of the three symbols of abundance and fecundity, expressed in the Chinese proverb, 'Many seeds, many sons.'

The ancient Greeks made the same associations, but at the same time knew it as the 'fruit of the dead', illustrating pomegranates' fundamental dualities across cultures – single and multiple, inside and out, death and immortality, excess and repentance, aphrodisiac and contraceptive.

This dual existence is encapsulated in the story of Hariti, celebrated in Japanese and Chinese Buddhism as the protective deity of childbirth and children. Hariti had one hundred children and was often depicted with a child in one arm and a pomegranate in the other. But in her past life, she was a child-devouring demoness, only able to find enlightenment as a consequence of eating a pomegranate. Some versions tell that Hariti stole other people's children to feed herself and her brood. The Buddha, of mind to teach her a lesson, hid one of her children under his rice bowl so that she would feel the loss as other mothers had. Distraught, she repented her child-eating ways and vowed to live on a diet of pomegranates.

The Greek of goddess of fertility, Rhea, is linked to the pomegranate, with some scholars recognizing her name (ῥέα) as the possible etymological metathesis (swapping of letters) from the old Homeric word for pomegranate (ῥόα). Rhea, a Titan, was the mother of the first generation of Olympian gods. Her descendants Aphrodite (goddess of love) and Hera (goddess of fertility and childbirth) inherited her affiliation with the pomegranate. It was Aphrodite who first planted a pomegranate tree on the island of Cyprus, where they now proliferate.

Much of the sorrow associated with the pomegranate comes from the tragedy of the virgin Persephone. Hades, god of the underworld, became infatuated with her and abducted her one day as she picked flowers. When her mother Demeter – the goddess of agriculture – learned that Zeus had allowed Persephone to be taken by his brother, she began to lay waste to crops. Forced to intervene, Zeus ordered Persephone's return. Hades agreed in principle, in the knowledge that the fates' law commanded if a person ate anything grown in the underworld, they could not leave. He gave Persephone a 'honey-sweet berry of the pomegranate', binding her to him.

An eventual compromise was decreed that Persephone, now the Queen of the Underworld, would live part of the year with Demeter and the rest with her husband, Hades. Much like the pomegranate, she had one foot in the light and one in the dark. When mother and daughter were reunited, the crops burst into life and when her daughter returned to the underworld the crops would wither – thus the seasons were established.

In another tragic Greek myth, a young girl called Side (σίδη), named after the Boeotian word for pomegranate, fled from her father's incestuous advances and took her own life at her mother's grave. As Side's blood seeped into the earth, a pomegranate tree grew, signifying their reunion and liberation from her oppressor.

These stories reflect the loss of innocence when girls are forced to transition into womanhood prematurely, as well as the separation of mother and daughter. In both, the pomegranate bridges the realms of the living and the dead.

In ancient Persia, pomegranates were considered one of the most sacred of all plants. The Zoroastrians associated them with the sun, planting them in their fire temples and burning the leaves in their ceremonies. Legendary hero Isfandiyar became invincible when he ate a pomegranate.

According to the ancient Greek historian Herodotus, the 'Persian Immortals' (an elite military force of 10,000 – so-called because of their ability to replenish their number instantly) wore gold or silver pomegranates on their spears. The outer 1,000 wore gold, and the enclosed 9,000 wore silver.

- Pomegranates play a key role in the ancient Persian festival of Yaldā Night, held on the winter solstice. The fruits symbolize life, light and health, in opposition to the darkness.
- Pomegranates are now considered a superfood, and it seems the ancient Egyptians thought so too, as they had a proverb: 'Eat a pomegranate and visit a bath; your youth will haste back.'

QUERCUS ROBUR

ENGLISH OAK

The oak tree holds a significant place in the folklore and mythology of its native regions. It is often described as having a connection to the gods, as being a source of magical power and even providing a home for fairies. In some cultures, these trees' striking personalities result in them taking human-like form. Both the Oak King of ancient Europe and the pagan Green Man (*see* COMMON HAWTHORN, p. 45) are embellished with the acorns, oak apples and the familiar lobed leaves.

The word 'druid' originates from an Irish-Gaelic word *doire*, meaning 'oak grove'. The druids venerated the oak and revered the cathedral-like space beneath the canopy as a place of worship and ceremony. When an oak died, the druids would strip the tree of its bark and erect it as a cross, pyramid or pillar for continued worship.

The relationship between oak and mistletoe was sacred. Mistletoe was considered a potently magical plant, used to ward off evil and intensify prayers and spells. Druids believed mistletoe was a gift from the gods, bestowed on the oak's limbs by way of lightning strikes. Oak-mistletoe was collected in old French and Swedish customs for its protective qualities.

Standing under an oak's sturdy boughs, it is hard to imagine anything could shake it. However, its very nature invites lightning; height, isolated position and high water content all make it a target. This relationship can be seen in folklore. Zeus, Jupiter and Thor – the lightning-wielding gods of thunder – are all closely affiliated with the oak. Jupiter, a god often crowned in oak leaves, is said to have taught the first men of Greece to take nourishment from the tree, earning them the name *balanophagy*, meaning acorn-eaters.

There is a German adage that translates as: 'Beeches you should seek, oaks you should avoid,' which may seem like sound advice in a thunderstorm, but it is in fact based on a false premise. Both trees are struck by lightning equally, but wet oak bark inadvertently channels the lightning into its trunk, resulting in visible and catastrophic damage. On the plus side, the splinters of a lightning-struck oak tree are said to alleviate toothache. Another old folk remedy claimed that silently rubbing a piece of oak on an open wound before sunrise on St John's Day (a celebration with both pagan and Christian origins in June) would hasten healing. In Germany, walking between the split of an oak was believed to be an effective hernia treatment.

Of the 600 or so species of *Quercus*, both deciduous and evergreen, almost all produce acorns, which symbolize birth, fertility and strength. In Norse folklore, the acorn represents the protective might of the tree. Placing an acorn on your windowsill protects your home. Likewise, carrying an acorn as a talisman is said to bestow vigour, youthfulness and determination.

Druids consumed acorns, believing that their prophetic qualities would allow them to divine the future. It is not only the acorn that can help with this task. Many oak trees were considered prophetic by Druids and Greco-Romans – for example, the oaks of the Dodona's Grove, where ancient Greek priests and priestesses would translate prophecies from the rustling leaves and the songs of the birds.

According to folklore, the contents of an oak apple (a gall formed on the oak's branches by the egg of the *Biorhiza pallida* wasp) can determine the success of the next crop yield (a worm indicates it will be good, a fly moderate and a spider poor, or nothing, which is very bad). However, historically, it is the tannins in the galls that have proved most useful, as they are one of the main ingredients in ink. It is poetic that much of the folklore in this chapter may have been penned with ink drawn from these remarkable spheres.

A fallen oak is a symbol of loss. Many people feel immensely protective over these friendly giants, imbuing them with memories and meaning. Gog and Magog are two ancient oaks in Glastonbury, Somerset in England. They are named after Britain's last surviving ancestors of the mythical pagan giants of old. They stand at what was once supposedly the beginning of a Druidic oak avenue leading up the Glastonbury Tor, which was then an island in the sea of Avalon. The Major Oak in Sherwood Forest, Nottinghamshire is a contender for Britain's largest oak, with a trunk circumference of 10 m (33 ft). Situated in the famed stomping grounds of Robin Hood, it is rumoured to have been a favoured camping spot of the outlaw and his band of merry men.

♦ Many a pub in Britain is named after the Royal Oak, which can be found in Staffordshire. The future King Charles II is said to have hidden in the tree while fleeing after the monarchy's defeat in the English Civil War.
♦ The boundary tree to the New Forest in Hampshire, England, was said to have come into green leaf on Old Christmas Day (6 January) in defiance of the country's change to the Gregorian calendar in 1752. Before the leaves could unfurl, they fell.
♦ The Latin name of the English oak, *Quercus robur*, literally translates to 'oak is strong.'

SALIX

WILLOW

There are more than 450 varieties of this tree, but it is the white willow (*Salix alba*) and the weeping willow (*Salix babylonica*) that are particularly present in folklore. Fast-growing and capable of taking root with ease, willow has earned a reputation for renewal, femininity, spring and rebirth. But it does have a spooky side, with a long-standing connection with death, grief and the occult.

The health benefits associated with willow bark were recognized by the Assyrians, as well as the ancient Egyptians and Greeks, and with good reason. Much later, in the eighteenth century, natural philosopher Edward Stone, drawing from the Doctrine of Signatures, theorized that the damp habitat of willow might make it effective in the treatment of fevers and rheumatoid arthritis. This approach was vindicated when he discovered salicylic acid in willow bark, a pain reliever and anti-inflammatory that was later synthesized into aspirin.

The willow was sacred to Persephone, Queen of the Underworld in ancient Greece, and it grew, alongside black poplar, at the entrance to the land of the dead. The power of protection that willow brought was harnessed by Orpheus, who, attempting to reclaim his wife Eurydice, entered the underworld carrying willow branches and a willow lyre. This was an effective strategy, as he was one of the very few mortals to survive the journey.

Greek witch-goddess Hecate carried a willow wand and was commemorated at her death with a grove of willows. Willow and witches are tied by many strands. The etymology of the neo-pagan religion Wicca may stem from an association with the bending and manipulating properties of willow.

Wicker is a method of weaving, whereby pliable twigs, usually willow, are used to make baskets and furniture. According to an old wives' tale, the best time to harvest the rods for weaving is during a waxing moon, and the worst during a waning moon. Some argue that the gravitational effects the moon has on the sap lends truth to this.

In the Somerset levels in England, where the flooded wetlands provided for a once-booming willow industry, there is an old folk belief that willows would stalk lonesome travellers late at night. Imagine how a traveller, senses muddled by the weight of the night upon their shoulders, would quake at a willow's looming silhouette, a gust of wind bringing the tree to life in a cacophony of whispers and sprawling branches. It might also reference the near visible speed with which a willow grows, no doubt inspiring J.R.R. Tolkien's ents (giant, tree-like beings) in *The Lord of the Rings* and J.K. Rowling's Whomping Willow (a violent magical tree) in *Harry Potter*.

Willow's relationship with grief and death originated in part with this appearance in Psalm 137 in the Bible: 'By the rivers of Babylon we sat and wept when we remembered Zion. There on the willows we hung our harps.'

This is, in fact, a case of mistaken identity, as the trees in question were likely Euphrates poplars. The weeping willow is also associated with the tears wept for Jesus Christ after his crucifixion. When palm was hard to come by, willow was used to make crosses on the Christian festival Palm Sunday. A willow cross kept in water was considered a charm to ward off disasters and thunder – but cutting willow on any day other than Palm Sunday was considered unlucky.

In Japan, weeping willows are thought to be haunted by apparitions. One particularly ghoulish tale tells of Yanagi onna – a mother and baby spirit, who appear at nighttime. The legend is that the pair were taking refuge from a storm when a branch whipped the mother, and they became entangled. Unable to escape the embrace of the willow, the pair were strangled, and their ghosts have haunted the trees ever since.

During sixteenth- and seventeenth-century Britain, the willow became a symbol of heartbreak and abandonment. Shakespeare's Ophelia, driven mad by the death of her father and Hamlet's rejection, fell out of a willow tree into the stream below and drowned underneath it. In the dating world, jilted gentlemen would wear a willow wreath as a sign of recent rejection. On the other hand, receiving a willow garland served as a callous indicator that you had been dumped.

♦ If a white willow is growing in a dry spot, it is a sure sign of an underground water source, which is perhaps why willow wood is often used to make divining rods.
♦ In Scotland, willow was used in the construction of gallows, leading to a superstition that using sawn willow timber for any other purpose would be an ill omen.
♦ In Louisiana, USA, it was said that when a willow's shade grew large enough to cover a grave, a family death would soon follow.

SAMBUCUS NIGRA

ELDER

To the superstitious, the elder is both friend and foe. On the one hand, 'God's stinking tree' (its nickname in parts of Dorset, England) carries associations with the devil and witches and is said to be the gruesome resting place of the biblical traitor Judas Iscariot, who some believe is to thank for its unappealing odour. The elder is often identified as the tree from which Judas hanged himself after his betrayal of Jesus, leading to Jesus's crucifixion. Some reports say that Judas was cut down before choking and, when 'falling headlong, his middle burst and his bowels poured forth.' The tree was forever marred by the traitor's gory demise, as the stench of his death was made permanent.

On the other hand, 'the medicine chest of country people' was believed by some, including the seventeenth-century English botanist John Evelyn and the German physician Michael Ettmüller, to be a 'catholicon' or cure-all. Their contemporary William Cole agreed, writing:

> There is hardly a disease from Head to Foot but it cures. It is profitable for the Headache, for Ravings and Wakings, Hypocondriack and Melancholy, the Falling-sicknesse, Catarrhs, Deafnesse, Faintnesse and Feacours.

Herr Ettmüller even doffed his cap to the tree whenever he passed one. The elder tree does indeed boast a plethora of folk remedies for nearly any ailment, from balding and shingles to warts and swellings. Wet elder leaves on a red cloth can treat haemorrhoids, and sticks in a rider's pocket will prevent saddle-sore.

During the eighteenth century, it was believed that drinking port would alleviate rheumatic symptoms, and at the time elderberries were used to enhance the flavour of cheaper versions. So effective was the ruse that the cultivation of the elder tree became illegal. But studies found it was the cheap elderberry-enhanced port that held real medicinal qualities, the top shelf stuff having no benefits whatsoever.

The somewhat unpleasant smell of the elder leaves acts as an effective fly deterrent, and so they were hung in dairies, bakeries, upon horse harnesses and even rubbed on to skin. A tree growing outside your back door, especially when self-seeded, was considered auspicious, and even better when coupled with a rowan growing out front. It would be wise, however, to keep your lawn well-raked, as there is also a folk belief that walking on top of elder leaves when pregnant could induce a miscarriage.

Elder has a strong affiliation with witches, who can stir a bucket of water with an elder stick to conjure a storm and transform into an elder branch to evade capture. In one story hailing from Northampton, England, a father cut off a branch for his son to play with and, to their shock, the tree bled profusely. Heading home, they encountered their neighbour wearing a blood-soaked bandage on her arm. It was a sign! The neighbour was a witch, and had been disguised as the tree. No doubt remained when she survived the 'swimming a witch' trial – only the innocent would drown.

It is said that sleeping under an elder, much like under a yew, is perilous, as the heavy aroma could send you into an unshakeable slumber. Burning it might bring forth the devil, who will scream and spit at you from its hot embers, ensuring any food cooked over it will be inedible.

Despite it being an ill omen to burn an elder, its name likely originates from the Anglo-Saxon word aeld, which means 'fire'. While the high water content in elder wood makes it poor firewood, the soft, inside core of the branches makes excellent kindling. As a by-product, the hollowed branches were popular for making instruments such as whistles and pipes for both humans and fairies alike.

As is common with white-blossomed trees (such as hawthorn, blackthorn and rowan), elder is associated with fairies, goddesses and female spirits. One of the most famous is the Danish tree spirit named Hyldemoer (Elder Mother). This Scandinavian matriarchal deity assumes the form of the tree. The Elder Mother is said to snuff out fires of elder sticks and curse furniture made from the wood; pinching babies in elder cradles, giving splinters on elder chairs and stunting children and animals with the strike of an elder cane. Only when absolutely necessary, a woodsman can ask Hyldemoer permission to cut an elder tree. He must kneel down in prayer position and recite thrice: 'Lady Elder, give me some of thy wood and I will give you some of mine when I become a tree.'

- According to a 17th-century British publication, standing under an elder tree at the peak of midsummer increases your chances of seeing a fairy.
- Elder's cycle of blossom and berry has been used to chart the English summer for centuries: summer is not here until the tree is fully in flower, and it ends when the berries are ripe.

SEQUOIA
SEMPERVIRENS

COAST REDWOOD

California's giants, the coast redwood (*Sequoia sempervirens*) and the giant sequoia (*Sequoiadendron giganteum*), are respectively the tallest and heaviest trees on Earth, growing upward of 100 m (328 ft) tall with trunks more than 8 m (26 ft) wide. General Sherman, a giant redwood and the heaviest tree on Earth, weighs more than ten blue whales. Hyperion, a coast redwood, stands at an extraordinary 116 m (380 ft). Hyperion was named after one of the twelve Greek Titans, born to Ouranos (Uranus, Heaven) and Gaia (Gaea, Earth) and means 'watcher from above'. Much of the folklore associated with the sequoia speaks of its steadfastness and goodwill – a tree trusted by the creator to live among humans, granting them guidance, strength and heart.

The genus *Sequoia* was named by botanist and linguist Stephan Endlicher in the mid-nineteenth century. It is a popular belief that Endlicher coined it in honour of a Cherokee named Sequoyah, who created the first Cherokee writing system at the beginning of the century. Sequoyah had observed how use of the written word by European settlers helped to preserve history and maintain cultural identity. At first, his syllabary was mistrusted – people associated it with witchcraft – but it was so effective that for a time, the literacy rates amongst the Cherokee exceeded that of the settlers.

In some Coast Miwok traditions, (an Indigenous people of California), the redwoods are elders of the first people. In some accounts, the mischievous creator Coyote stood on top of Sonoma Mountain and waved a tule (bulrush) blanket, drying out the surrounding waters to form land. He created the first people, from whom all people, animals and plants were made. The elders of the first people were given the form of coast redwoods, adopting the colour red as a reminder of their blood and heritage. As the trees spread west, they grew even taller, so that everyone would see their rich, red colour and be reminded of their story and origins.

Another Californian Indigenous people – the Yurok – call the giant redwoods 'po-po-leen', which is the same word used to describe their elders. An interpretation of the Yurok creation story speaks of the kindness of the redwood. Before humans were created, in a time when animals and plants could speak freely with one another, a family of little brown birds prepared to migrate south. One of the birds was injured but bravely told his family to go without him. He waved them off with a smile and started to look for a tree that could offer him shelter until the cold season passed, whistling hopefully as he went.

The first tree was a dogwood. It declined, concerned that the bird might damage its beautiful blossom. The alder was too busy. Even the oak turned the bird away. Disheartened and afraid, the bird bowed his head and wandered down the Klamath River, his tune turned melancholy.

Above, a redwood with its giant heart was moved by the lonely song. The bird stumbled against the enormous roots and looked up in awe. Summoning all his courage, he asked if he could take shelter in the tree's branches. The coast redwood bent down and gently lifted up the injured bird. The bird told the tree of his growing longing for his family and, in response, the tree showed the bird the view from its tallest branch. Pointing to the surrounding trees, he promised the little bird that when his family returned, they would all find a home atop the redwoods with their warm hearts.

The creator was touched by the kindness of the redwoods. Later, when he created humans, he asked the redwoods to look after them and provide timber for their canoes and shelters. (Indeed for thousands of years, the Yurok people have made their homes and canoes from fallen redwoods. The canoes are hand-carved to include physical representations of the heart, lungs and kidneys, and are afforded the same respect as any person within the community.) The small-minded trees that had turned down the little bird were taught to value community over vanity and ego. The dogwood would only flower for a short season, the alder would unburden itself of its leaves so it could find time to help others, and the oak would produce acorns so the Yurok could make flour. The little bird (now known as the marbled murrelet) would no longer need to migrate south, instead wintering in the welcoming branches of the redwood.

Old-growth coast redwoods can live for well over 2,000 years, sating their thirst with thick fog that rolls in from the Pacific Ocean. Although their height makes them vulnerable to lightning strikes, their thick, fibrous bark insulates the tree within. Thick blankets of charcoal can be seen on lightning-struck trees. If a fire is ferocious enough to irreparably damage the redwood, new growth can sprout from its root system, creating enchanting circles of redwoods known as fairy rings.

SORBUS
AUCUPARIA

ROWAN

Rowan, also referred to as mountain ash or witchwood, is a small yet resilient tree. Its bright red or orange berries, technically known as pomes, add vibrant colour to the often-challenging environments in which it thrives. A vestige of the old flower, the pomes bare a pentagram shape on their base – a symbol of protection and perfection throughout superstition, and no other tree rivals the rowan as a protective ward, especially against witchcraft and the evil eye. Cradles were made of rowan to ward away evil, and walking sticks would prevent the owner from becoming lost or 'fairy led'.

Today witchwood trees are often found near thresholds to dwellings and other structures. In seventeenth- and eighteenth-century Yorkshire (in England) it was believed that witches could outmanoeuvre the trees situated at the threshold by flying down the chimney, prompting the erection of rowan 'witch posts' at either end of a hearth.

The protective qualities of the wood were often employed in dairies, to prevent witches from souring butter or milk. In Germany, butter paddles were crafted from rowan, while an Irish folk ritual – described in a collection of folklore compiled by R. Clarke in 1882 – suggested that on the morning of the pagan festival Beltane (May Day), cows should be 'struck with a quicker-berry [Rowan] switch, which prevents any person putting any evil on them or taking their profit or butter', and so 'the milk rose in the udder as the sap in the stick'. Another Irish superstition was that the first household to light a fire on Beltane morning would be vulnerable to witches looking to steal their luck and milk profits. A clever trick was to hang dried rowan leaves above the fire, as the smoke would prevent witches from entering.

In a once-popular ritual (something of a pagan/Christian lovechild), superstitious people would craft an equal-armed rowan cross to tuck into their pocket or clothes lining, in the belief that 'Rowan tree and red thread, make the witches tine [lose] their speed', according to an old Scottish incantation. However, there were some rules to follow: the maker must vary their outward and returning route to the rowan tree, the cross must be made without the aid of metal tools, and the wood must not be taken from the same rowan tree twice.

In Irish myth, fairies loved rowan berries. One day, a berry dropped into the realm of humans and grew into a giant rowan tree. The tree's berries were believed to be magical: one berry would get you drunk, two would grant you one hundred years of life and three would keep you at the age of thirty for that century. The fairies employed a one-eyed giant called Searbhán to guard the coveted berries, but he met his match in 'The Pursuit of Diarmuid and Gráinne', a tale from the Fianna Cycle of Irish mythology. This tells the story of the love triangle between legendary hero Fionn mac Cumhaill, the beautiful princess Gráinne and her paramour Diarmuid. Gráinne, once destined to marry Fionn, eloped with Diarmuid. Encountering the magic rowan tree, the pregnant Gráinne developed a craving for its berries. This angered Searbhán and a fight ensued, but Diarmuid used the one-eyed giant's club to defeat him.

As the lovers feasted on the sweetest berries atop the rowan, Fionn and his warriors appeared. Upon seeing the slain giant, Fionn knew that only Diarmuid was capable of such a feat and so must be nearby. He set up camp under the tree and, to pass the time, challenged a warrior to a Fidchell match (a chess-like game). Diarmuid, who was an able player, threw berries from his hiding place to indicate the correct moves for Fionn's opponent. Beaten, Fionn realized again that it must have been the work of Diarmuid and started searching the boughs of the tree. But before he could capture the pair, the god of love Óengus intervened and helped them escape.

In a Finnish creation myth, the goddess Rauni (*reynir*, rowan in old Norse) came down to a barren Earth in the form of a mountain ash. Rauni conceived all plants when her husband Ukko, the thunder god, struck her with his lightning bolt.

As for the rowan tree's unique characteristics, there is an explanation drawn from Greek mythology, though not referenced in classical literature. When the reckless goddess of youth Hebe lost her chalice containing the elixir of eternal youth, the gods sent a mighty eagle to retrieve the chalice from some dastardly demons. After a fraught and bloodied battle, the chalice was retrieved, but the battleground was strewn with the eagle's blood and feathers, from which the first rowans grew – with blood-red berries and serrated 'feather-shaped' leaves.

+ In Scotland, a christened man could mark a witch by tapping her with a stick of rowan, flagging her for collection by the devil.
+ The Celts called mountain ash *fid na ndruad* (wizards' tree) and it represents the second letter of the Ogham alphabet.

TAXUS BACCATA

YEW

The yew, ominous and densely branched, is the longest living native tree in Britain and possibly northern Europe. Frequently found in graveyards and almost entirely poisonous, it has embedded itself as a sombre motif of mourning within folklore for millennia.

In British folklore, however, the yew is redeemed by its associations with resurrection, perhaps thanks to its evergreen foliage, extraordinary lifespan, self-rooting branches and rejuvenating properties. Yew trees and churches often stand together, overseers of a rapidly changing world, and in more than 500 English churchyards, the yew outdates the church itself. The Celts believed the roots of the yew granted access to the afterlife, and they would often build places of worship beside the arboreal conduits. Christians likely appropriated these locations when erecting their churches and embraced the yews. The tree was said to thrive in soil filled with the dead and absorbed the putrefaction and disease of their remains – possibly why they were planted on the graves of plague victims. Another folk belief was the roots would grow through the eye sockets of the dead, anchoring them below ground lest they tried to escape. For the living, their presence in churchyards also acted as a deterrent, giving farmers pause before allowing their livestock to wander on to holy ground.

The aril (the red, fleshy cup around each seed) of the yew is the only part that is not toxic. The rest of the tree is so poisonous that as little as 50 g (1.8 oz) may prove fatal. In Shakespeare's *Macbeth*, the three witches use a yew-sprig to concoct a poison, alongside their famous incantation. There is a myth that if you doze off beneath a yew tree, you will never wake. While it is probably perfectly safe to shelter under a yew, it is prudent to take great care when picnicking below its bows.

In one Welsh tale, a weary young farmhand and his friend took a nap under a yew. When the man awoke, his friend had disappeared. It transpired that the ground beneath the yew was a portal to the Tylwyth Teg, realm of the fairy folk. On advice from the village sage, the farmhand found him exactly one year later, dancing with the supernaturals under the same tree. The farmhand pulled his friend out to find him a shadow of his former self. The friend was surprised by the farmhand's concern – surely he had not been dancing for long, scarcely an evening?! But the moment he was given something to eat in a bid to regain his strength, he turned to dust and died.

In the first edition of *Britannia* – a historical survey of Great Britain and Ireland, published in 1586 – scholar William Camden documented a theory about the expansion and renaming of a small village previously known as Horton. A clergyman became infatuated with a local maid, but when his advancements were rejected, he chopped off her head and tossed it to the roadside in a pique of rage. The head then became lodged in a twisting yew branch, with its hair tangled in the tree. Over time, the bark grew around the maiden's hair, giving the tree its unique fibrous quality. The tree became venerated and a popular site of pilgrimage, as visitors from far and wide arrived to pull at the bark and foliage in hopes of obtaining good fortune. Such was the popularity that the village grew into a substantial town and was renamed in Old English as *Halig-fax* (Halifax), meaning 'holy hair'.

Britain is home to two contenders for the title of oldest tree in Europe. In Fortingall, Aberfeldy you can find a yew claimed to be 3,000 years old at the birth of Jesus Christ (and so over 5,000 years old today). A male tree, it captivated scientists in 2015 when a female branch, clad with red arils, appeared. And in St George's churchyard in Crowhurst, Surrey you can find an enormous and ancient specimen with a wooden door at the entrance to its hollowed interior. In 1820, villagers found a cannonball inside which may have been there since the English Civil War (1642–51).

♦ The panelled door of St Edward's Church in Stow-on-the-Wold, Cheltenham, England, is flanked by two dramatic yews that have fused to the stone wall. The evocative sight supposedly inspired J.R.R. Tolkien's famous 'Doors of Durin' in *The Lord of the Rings*.

♦ St Mary's Church in Painswick, Gloucestershire, England, accommodates ninety-nine yew trees. Legend stipulates that if a hundredth were to take root, the Devil would pluck it from the soil.

♦ The Bleeding Yew at Nevern Church in Pembrokeshire, Wales, is famous for producing dark red sap. Some say it weeps for an innocent monk hanged for a crime he did not commit, while others say it bleeds for world peace.

THEOBROMA CACAO

CACAO

Despite its modest size and tendency to grow in the shade of other trees, the cacao has an immense and profound legacy. Its genus name, *Theobroma*, derives from the ancient Greek for 'food of the gods'. For the Mesoamericans, where the tree originated, its fruiting pods were indeed divine gifts.

Cacao trees were first discovered by the Mokaya and Olmec people of the Gulf of Mexico's coast. Little written history survives, but vessels containing traces of cacao speak of its cultural value. Fermented beans and pulp would be mixed with water, cinnamon and possibly red chilli to make a drink that would foam when poured from a height. It was believed that within the foam was the essence of God – the foamier the beverage, the greater the maker's worth. The drink was used ceremoniously in marriage, death and other celebrations, and was associated with fertility. These ancient traditions continued through the Maya and Aztec civilizations, with some Maya brides expected to demonstrate their pouring skills at their own weddings.

Along with maize, cacao is central in the Maya origin story, as written in the sacred text of the *Popol Vuh*. In the beginning, when there was only sky and sea, skilled ball-player god Hun Hunahpu was playing above the underworld. The gods below were angered by the noise and lured him down under the pretence of playing a game. Too late, Hun realized he had been deceived, and the gods of the underworld sacrificed him. From Hun's body the first cacao tree is said to have burst. When the gods hung his decapitated head on the tree as a trophy, a maiden of the underworld passed by and stopped for a chat. Hun's head spat on her hand, causing a set of twins to be conceived in her womb.

The Maya Hero Twins grew to be formidable ball players, like their father. Seeking revenge for his death, the twins decided to play a game on the same court, above the gods of the underworld. Again, the gods invited them down but they were prepared for the trick and exacted their revenge, killing the gods. Their father's spirit was able to ascend from his body beneath the cacao tree and out of the underworld, reemerging as the maize god. The twins were elevated into the sky, becoming the sun and the moon. With the arrival of these celestial bodies, the gods were able to grow corn, and from that they were able to create humans.

The Toltecs, who were predecessors of the Aztecs, told of Quetzalcoatl's generosity to the mortals. After the plumed serpent god presented the Toltecs with plants of sustenance (corns, beans and yucca), he stole a cacao tree from the gods, to give to them. But the theft did not go unnoticed, and the gods punished Quetzalcoatl, tricking him into getting drunk. Quetzalcoatl fled in shame, never to be seen again, but not before planting his final cacao seeds for his mortal friends.

The Aztecs adopted the Toltec gods and carried forward their mythology. In another cacao origin story, a respected princess was besieged by her husband's adversaries during his absence. The men demanded that she reveal her husband's treasure, but the faithful princess remained silent until her death. Quetzalcoatl was so moved by her honour that from her blood the first cacao plant was born; the bitter flesh representing her suffering love, and the true treasure, the seeds, a reflection of her virtue.

The Aztecs called their frothy cacao drink xocolatl (meaning bitter drink). Consumption of cacao was more of an elite pastime than it had been in the Maya civilization. Outvaluing gold, it was considered a symbol of power, offered in tribute to Aztec rulers. Ruler Montezuma II was said to have drunk fifty cups a day in order to maintain his energy and sexual vigour.

The Spanish conquest of the Americas resulted in the gradual introduction of cacao to Europe, but when sugar cane was added to the beverage in the sixteenth century, its popularity rose sharply. During the nineteenth century, solid chocolate bars were developed and milk added to the recipe. The delicacy became a confectionery giant and 'cocoa' (a misspelling) is now an essential ingredient in the multibillion-pound chocolate industry.

Recently there has been a revival of cacao ceremonies, with spiritual rituals harking back to the Mesoamerican roots. The social gatherings are said to improve mindfulness and foster creativity and togetherness – cacao consumption is known to release dopamine and endorphins, alleviating symptoms of depression.

ZIZIPHUS

JUJUBE

The Islamic Sidr tree, which marks the boundary of angels and ascension, also provided the materials to craft Jesus's crown of thorns, which snagged upon his head during his crucifixion in the Bible.

While other trees such as holly (*see* p. 73) and hawthorn (*see* p. 45) have laid claim to being Jesus's crown of thorns, the small, sweet-fruiting and heavily thorned jujube, *Ziziphus spina-christi* (Christ's thorn), is the most likely candidate, as it grows prodigiously around Jerusalem. A relic purporting to be the original crown, accompanied by a section of the cross and a nail that held Jesus in place on the cross, still exists today. As early as 407 CE, this crown was already described by the Roman poet Paulinus of Nola as a revered relic. Later, it spent 500 years in Sainte-Chapelle, France, under the ownership of King Louis IX, and was transferred to Notre-Dame in 1806, where it survived the 2019 fire. At the time of the crucifixion, the jujube thorns would have been interwoven into a wreath made of Baltic rush, but they have been removed over the years and presented as highly prized religious artifacts. One thorn owned by Mary Queen of Scots (1542–87) still exists, wrapped in her pearls.

In the Qu'ran, *Ziziphus spina-christi* is referred to as the Sidr tree. One in particular, Sidrat al-Muntaha (the Sidr tree at the farthest boundary) marks the edge of the seventh heaven, where the knowledge of the angels ends.

During Muhammad's quest to meet with Allah (God), the Archangel Gabriel accompanied him as far as the tree. From there, Muhammad continued alone, receiving visions and instruction from Allah of the five daily prayers (Salah).

In an old Muslim legend, a many-leaved jujube grows in Paradise and each living person on Earth has a leaf bearing their name. During Ramadan, the tree shudders, dropping a portion of its leaves to make way for new ones. Those whose leaves fall to the ground will pass that year, and the speed of the leaf's decay mirrors the rapidity of their decline.

One ancient jujube snag (standing dead tree) in the biblical city of Al-Qurnah in southern Iraq, is locally revered as the Tree of Knowledge, once said to have stood in the Garden of Eden along with the Tree of Life. This belief came from a geographic reference in the Bible that stated that Eden was situated at the meeting point of the rivers of Pishon, Havilah, Tigris and Euphrates. Most likely the geography has changed significantly since then, but the tree's location does mark the confluence of the Tigris and the Euphrates.

Cutting down a jujube early is believed to bring swift, certain death. A tree harmed is said to gush blood-red sap and groan in anguish. But for most, the tree is thought to ward off demons and its protective qualities make it a safe place to sleep. Near the Al-Jazzar mosque in Israel there was a jujube that grew unusually large for a typically small species. Over time, its expansive roots started to disturb nearby graves and so in 2000 the decision was made to fell the tree to protect the sanctity of the dead. During the felling, clumps of iron nails were discovered lodged in its trunk, a leftover from a ritual partaken by Muslim women hoping to repel the evil eye. These women walked to and from the tree in absolute silence. At its trunk, they struck the nails into the tree with calls of 'Allahu akbar' from the mosques. Thus the women exorcised themselves of any curses that they may have been victim to.

For Hindus as well, the jujube has significance in myth and legend. The sweet fruit of *Ziziphus mauritiana* (or the Indian jujube) is a favoured delicacy of Hindu deities Saraswati (goddess of knowledge) and Shiva (the destroyer). In the Bengal region, it is customary to avoid eating a *kul* or *ber* (jujube fruits) before the Saraswati Puja festival, so that the goddess can receive her share first. This practice also dissuades children from eating the fruits before they are ripe.

Badrinath, meaning 'lord of the jujube tree' is an epithet of the Hindu god Vishnu. One time when Vishnu was meditating in the Himalayas, the goddess Lakshmi, Vishnu's consort, took the form of the jujube and provided fruit to sustain the deity, who had been taken off guard by the inclement weather. In thanks to Lakshmi and the jujube, Vishnu named the place Badarikashrama, 'the place with the badari tree', which continues to be a destination for pilgrims.

A favourite Hindu legend tells of a hunter's daughter, Shabari, who was dismayed by violence inflicted on animals and left her home in search of wisdom and knowledge. On her way, she encountered a benevolent sage named Matanga, who offered her a prophetic blessing, foreseeing her meeting with Lord Rama (the seventh incarnation of Vishnu). From that moment, Shabari dedicated her life to that eventuality, collecting jujube fruits as an offering for when they met. When the day eventually came, Shabari gave Lord Rama her gift, but only after taking a bite from each one herself. Instead of horror at her insolence, Rama was profoundly moved. He realized she was tasting each fruit to prevent him eating any sour ones. While he was indifferent to the calibre of the gift, her devotion was such that he granted her immediate liberation and ascension from the mortal realm.

Acknowledgements

I owe a great gratitude to Leaping Hare Press and Quarto for publishing my first solo book, especially to the commissioning editor Sophie Lazar, who showed great faith in and a shared vision for the book. And editor Katerina Menhennet and senior designer Renata Latipova for their expertise and patience.

A huge thanks to my family and friends – my parents, who took my sons on countless trips to Dunster Castle; my wife, Hannah Bailey, who while seamlessly juggling her career as an illustrator alongside motherhood, still found time to read through every word of this book: her first round of edits were invaluable. And of course thank you to my two sons, Edwyn and Ivor, who charmingly slowed the whole process down, effortlessly bringing me back down to Earth.

Thank you to Rod Harrington, my village tree warden, who lent me many books and sang me songs about trees in his front room.

And finally, thank you to the trees and their storytellers, whose relationships have inspired so much in humanity, least of all this book.

For further reading ideas, go to
www.thefolkloreoftrees.com

Also available in the series:

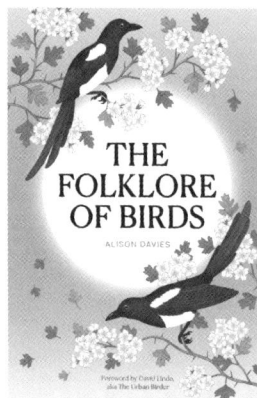

THE
FOLKLORE
OF BIRDS

ALISON DAVIES

Foreword by David Lindo,
aka The Urban Birder

About the author and illustrator

Aidan Meighan is an author, illustrator and arboreal devotee living in Somerset, England, with a passion for nature and storytelling. For fifteen years, Aidan has been passionately drawing trees, maps and beautiful places from around the world in his distinctive style, working with travel and lifestyle books and magazines, brands and destinations. Aidan is an enthusiast for the written word and print, and has been instrumental in the production of the *Glastonbury Free Press* newspaper since its inception in 2013. He is also a keen gardener and back-yard conservationist. His first book, *The Folklore of Trees*, is a joyful coming together of Aidan's passions and interests. You can find Aidan on his website, www.aidanmeighan.com, and on Instagram, @aidan_meighan.

About the Foreword author

Extraordinarily creative and prolific, **Chris Packham** has led a remarkable life. He's gained recognition as a naturalist, television presenter, writer, photographer, conservationist, campaigner and filmmaker. He is best known for his environmental and animal welfare activism. His TV credits include 'Springwatch' and 'Earth' for the BBC, and 'Is It Time to Break the Law?' for Channel 4. Alongside his ambassadorial roles for numerous NGOs, he runs independent campaigns aimed at nature recovery and ending animal cruelty. Chris is also a vocal advocate for neurodiversity, with a special focus on autism. His mantras are 'winning is not giving up' and 'shout above the noise'.

Index

Quarto

First published in 2026 by Leaping Hare Press,
an imprint of The Quarto Group.
One Triptych Place, London, SE1 9SH,
United Kingdom
T (0)20 7700 9000
www.Quarto.com

EEA Representation, WTS Tax d.o.o., Žanova ulica 3, 4000 Kranj, Slovenia
www.wts-tax.si

A catalogue record for this book is available from the British Library.

ISBN 978-1-83600-855-2
Ebook ISBN 978-1-83600-856-9

10 9 8 7 6 5 4 3 2 1

Illustrations by Aidan Meighan
Design by Dinah Drazin
Editorial Director: Monica Perdoni
Commissioning Editor: Sophie Lazar
Senior Designer: Renata Latipova
Editor: Katerina Menhennet
Senior Production Controller: Rohana Yusof

Printed in Guangdong, China TT112025